WILD WEATHER
Storms, Meteorology, and Climate

T0018141

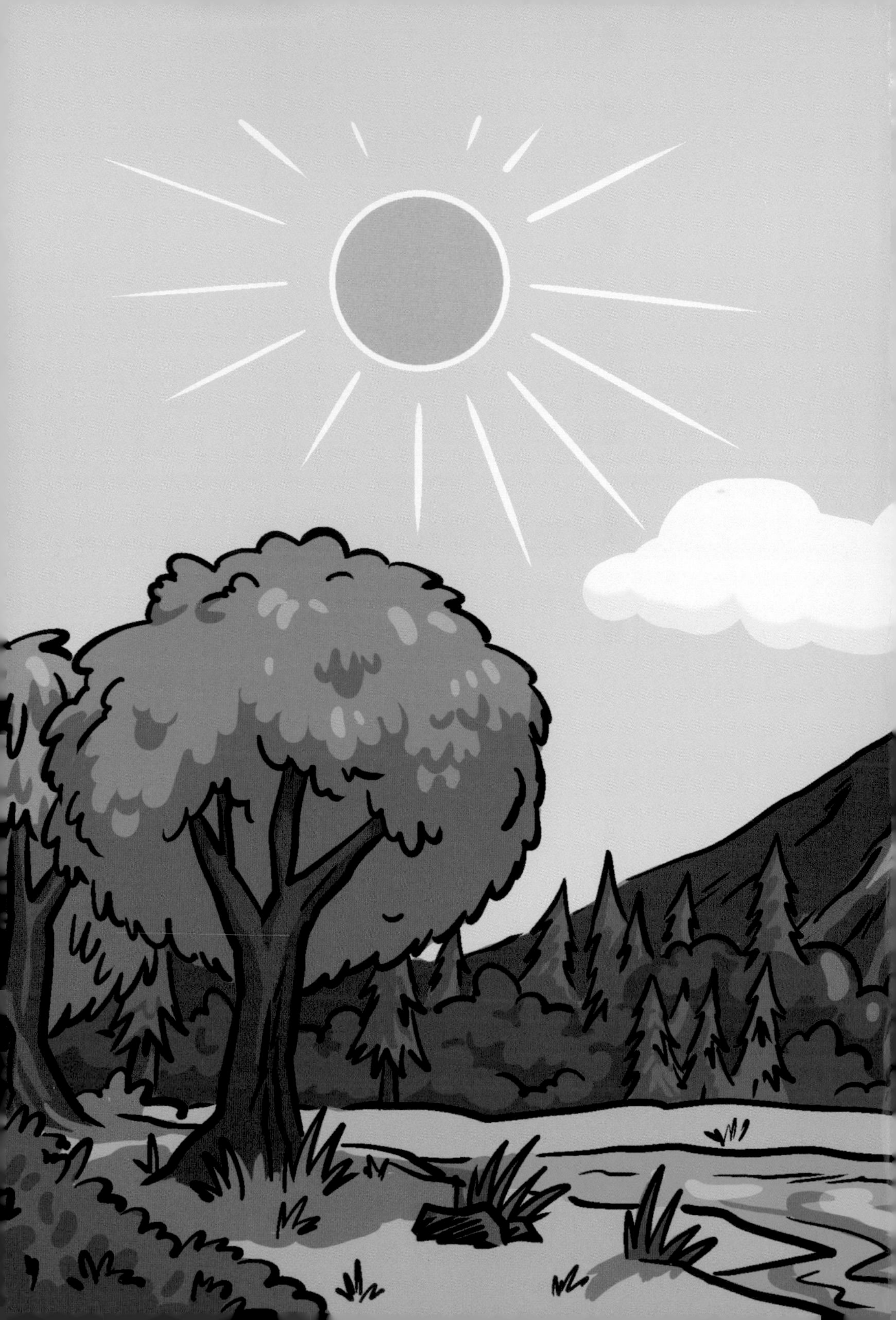

WILD WEATHER

Storms, Meteorology, and Climate

written by
MK REED

illustrated by
JONATHAN HILL

with color by
NYSSA ORU

:01

First Second

New York

To local news stations everywhere and in particular Matt Zaffino on KGW, the best meteorologist in the Portland Metro area.
—Jonathan

First Second

Text copyright © 2019 by MK Reed
Illustrations copyright © 2019 by Jonathan Hill

Don't miss your next favorite book from First Second! For the latest updates go to firstsecondnewsletter.com and sign up for our enewsletter.

Drawn in Clip Studio Paint EX with the Frenden brushes Red Real Pencil for the pencils and The Natural for the inks. Digitally colored in Procreate and Photoshop. Lettered in ComicCrazy.

Published by First Second
First Second is an imprint of Roaring Brook Press,
a division of Holtzbrinck Publishing Holdings Limited Partnership
120 Broadway, New York, NY 10271

Library of Congress Control Number: 2018938084

Paperback ISBN: 978-1-62672-790-8
Hardcover ISBN: 978-1-62672-789-2

Our books may be purchased in bulk for promotional, educational, or business use. Please contact your local bookseller or the Macmillan Corporate and Premium Sales Department at (800) 221-7945 ext. 5442 or by e-mail at MacmillanSpecialMarkets@macmillan.com.

First edition, 2019
Edited by Dave Roman
Book design by John Green
Meteorology consultant: Alicia Wasula

Printed in China by Toppan Leefung Printing Ltd., Dongguan City, Guangdong Province
Paperback: 10 9
Hardcover: 10 9 8 7 6 5

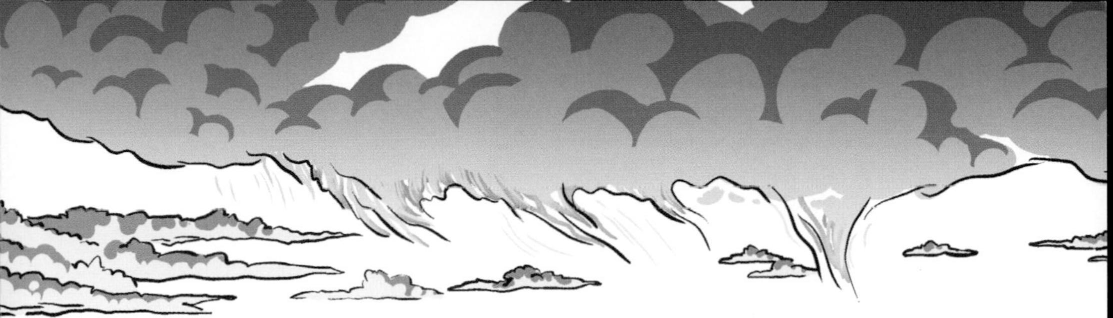

Weather can be amazing, exciting, fascinating, and terrifying . . . sometimes all at the same time! When the weather is nice and tranquil, you might not think too much about it. But when lightning darts across the sky or when high winds shake and rattle your house, weather may be the *only* thing you're thinking about.

I first realized the power of weather when I was seven years old, watching a TV show at home on a warm, humid spring night. Suddenly the broadcast was interrupted by a very serious-looking weathercaster. She pointed to a big blob on a radar and told us that our city was under a tornado warning. Was I scared? Absolutely. But I was also curious. How did this weathercaster know there was a tornado coming? And how did she stay so *calm*? I dashed across the house to let my parents know about the warning, and then I took a very quick look at those dark churning clouds. Right then, I knew I wanted to learn as much as I could about tornadoes. Before long, I was also interested in everything else about weather. I ended up studying meteorology in college and taking part in severe-storm research. So my life took a big turn on that dark and stormy night!

Most of my work these days involves writing about weather and climate, but I once got to spend a whole summer on the road as part of a research project, keeping an eye on the big thunderstorms of eastern Colorado (not in the mountains, but on the Great Plains). Our mission was to document what these storms were doing—raining, hailing, sometimes even producing twisters—and report back to the National Weather Service so they could fine-tune a new Doppler radar system. It was amazing to witness the power of the atmosphere day after day, but I also learned how challenging it can be to predict thunderstorms behavior and how difficult it can be to drive safely when you're surrounded by hazardous weather. Even trained professionals can get into

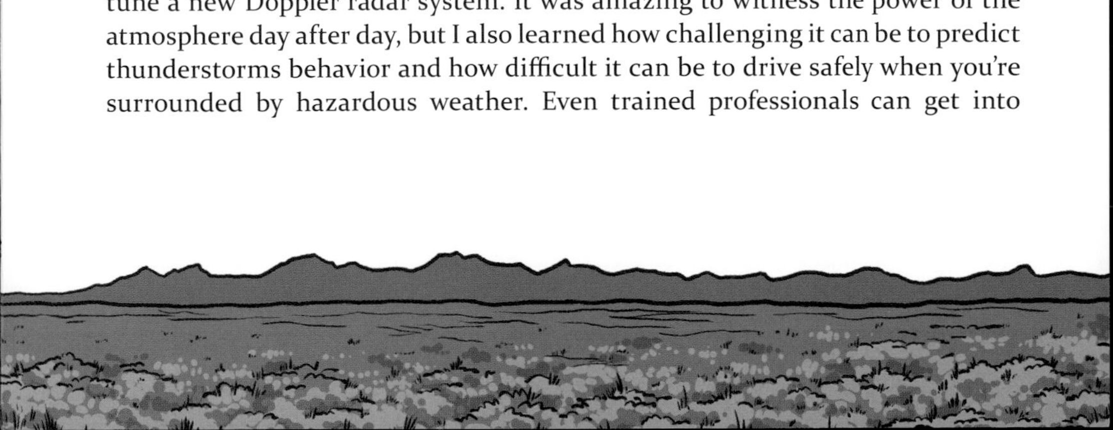

trouble when they chase storms, which is why it's best to watch the spectacular "sky shows" that nature gives us from a safe vantage point.

One of the great things about weather is it's free! The only equipment you *really* need to appreciate the atmosphere are your own senses. Even if you don't have a weather station, you can keep a "weather diary" and take note of what you see, hear, and feel every day. Sometimes the air feels like a soft, warm blanket—and sometimes it feels more like a thousand needles trying to pierce your skin. The wind can sound like a gentle whistle or a screaming blast. And there's an ever-changing parade of clouds, light, and texture in the sky above.

Even though weather is right in front of us all the time, the atmosphere can still feel mysterious. In this book, you'll find out many things scientists have learned about weather over the years: why we have seasons, why it rains and snows, what makes the wind blow, how hurricanes get named, why an EF5 tornado is so much worse than an EF1, and much more. Since hurricanes and tornadoes can be truly frightening, it's good that we have powerful tools, like radars and satellites, that keep track of wild weather from a safe distance. Forecasters at the National Weather Service and broadcast meteorologists like Stormin' Norman Weatherby—who you'll meet in this book—work hard to keep us informed about dangerous storms. Looking further out, we can now predict the weather days ahead of time with more and more skill, thanks to the help of computer programs that analyze the atmosphere and project it further into the future.

There's something else that many atmospheric scientists are examining: the impact of greenhouse gases on our weather and climate. Every time we burn coal, oil, or gas, we put heat-trapping gases into the air. These gases have now accumulated enough to raise global temperatures and to make heavy rains even heavier. What will our changing climate bring as your own lifetime

unfolds? What can we do to adjust to these changes? And how can we slow down the accumulation of greenhouse gases to help limit the changes to our atmosphere?

You can help! The world needs people with many different skills to analyze weather and climate and to keep everyone safe and well-informed. If you enjoy computing, you might help write the programs that track the atmosphere and predict what it will do next. If you like math and physics, you could become a research scientist, investigating one of the many yet-to-be-solved mysteries of our atmosphere. You might become an engineer, helping to design and build the next weather satellite. Do you enjoy teamwork? We need folks to organize big research projects all over the world and to help people transition toward cleaner energy. If you like to explain things, you could write articles to make weather and climate science easy to understand. You might even find yourself giving tomorrow's forecast on TV or on a smartphone, just like Stormin' Norman.

Weather is something you can enjoy and learn about your whole life. One man named Richard Hendrickson kept track of the weather on Long Island, New York, from age 18 until he was 101. That's more than 80 years! Thousands of volunteers like Richard collect weather observations every day and send them to the National Weather Service. Whether you're watching the sky as a scientist, a volunteer observer, or an everyday weather lover, I hope you find the atmosphere as exciting and awesome as I do.

—Robert Henson,
meteorologist and science writer,
coauthor of *Meteorology Today*,
and author of *The Thinking Person's Guide to Climate Change*

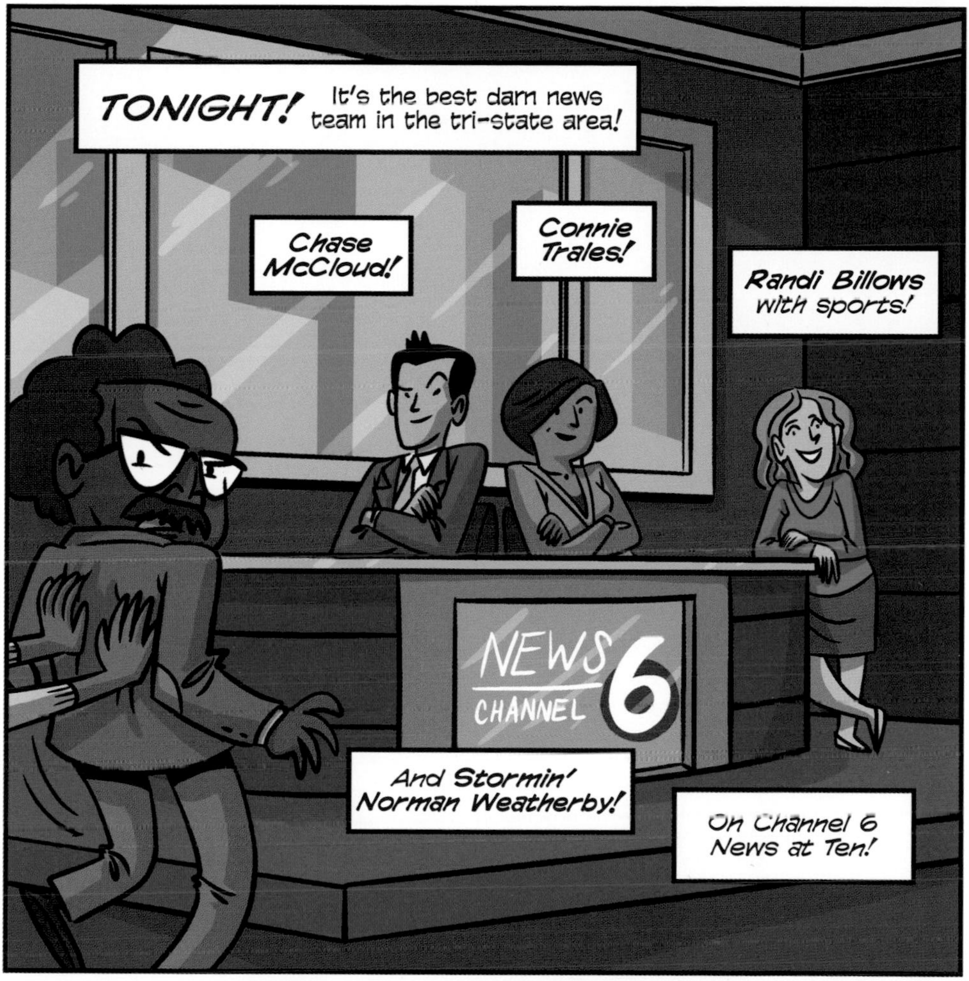
TONIGHT! It's the best darn news team in the tri-state area!
Chase McCloud!
Connie Trales!
Randi Billows with sports!
NEWS CHANNEL 6
And Stormin' Norman Weatherby!
On Channel 6 News at Ten!

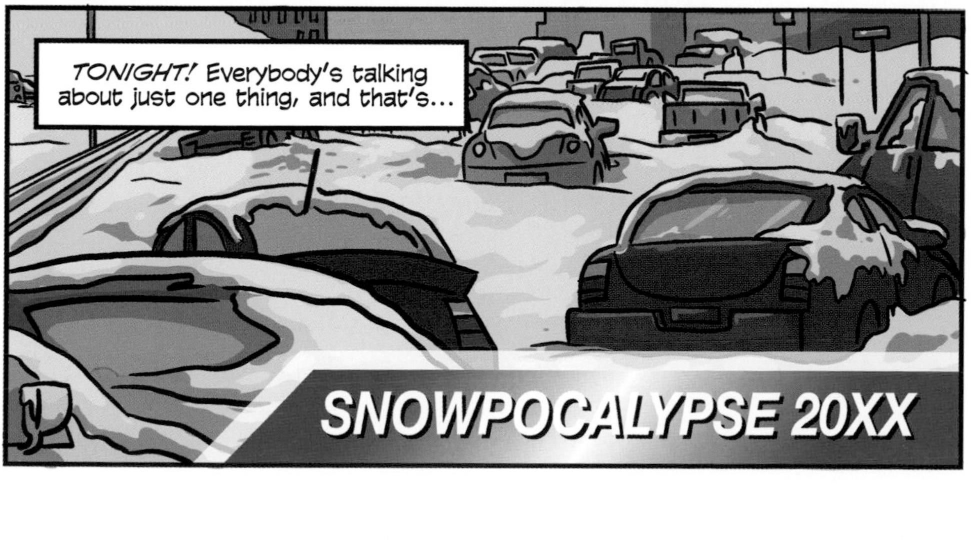
TONIGHT! Everybody's talking about just one thing, and that's...
SNOWPOCALYPSE 20XX

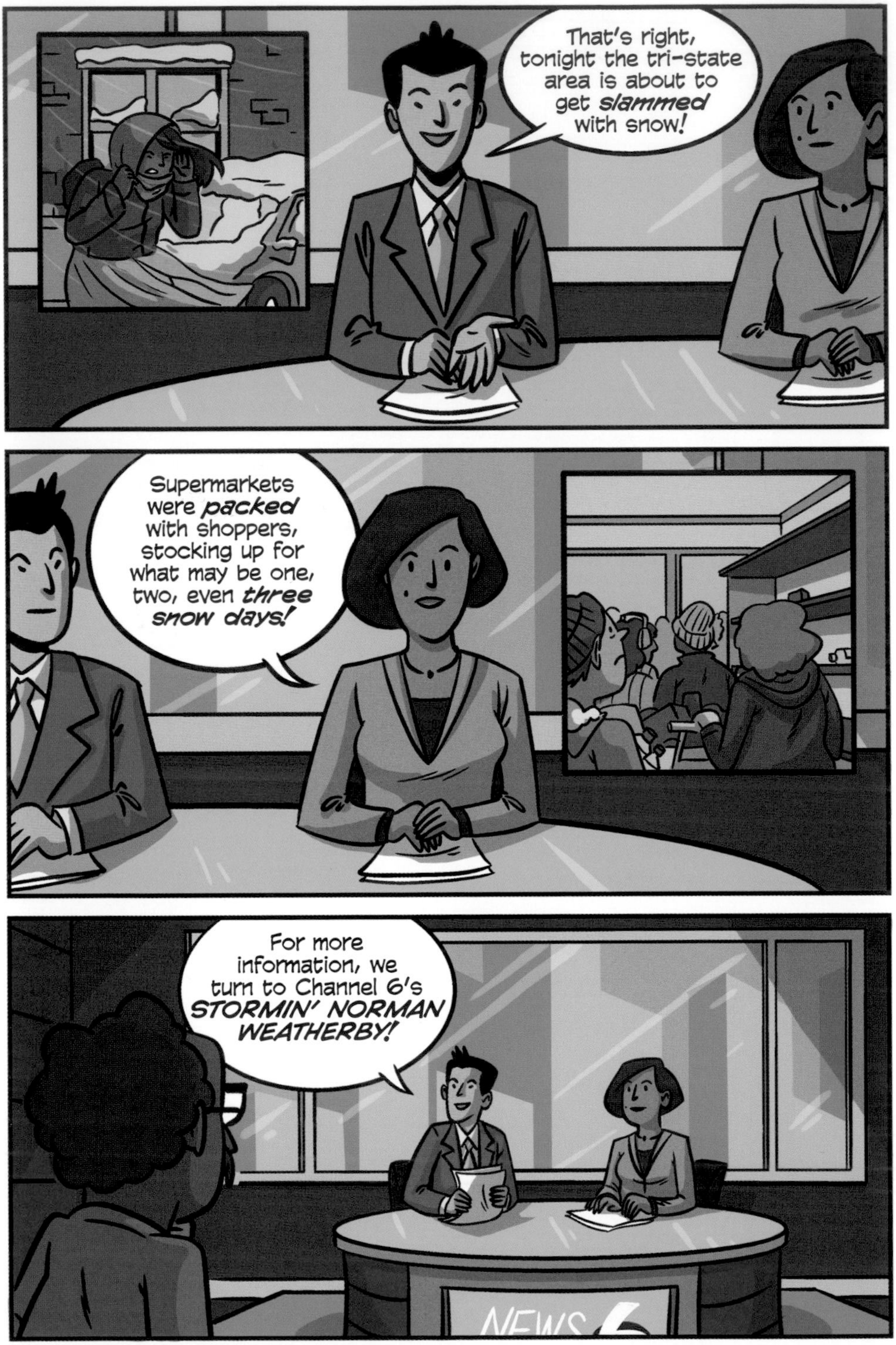
That's right, tonight the tri-state area is about to get *slammed* with snow!
Supermarkets were *packed* with shoppers, stocking up for what may be one, two, even *three snow days!*
For more information, we turn to Channel 6's *STORMIN' NORMAN WEATHERBY!*
NEWS 6

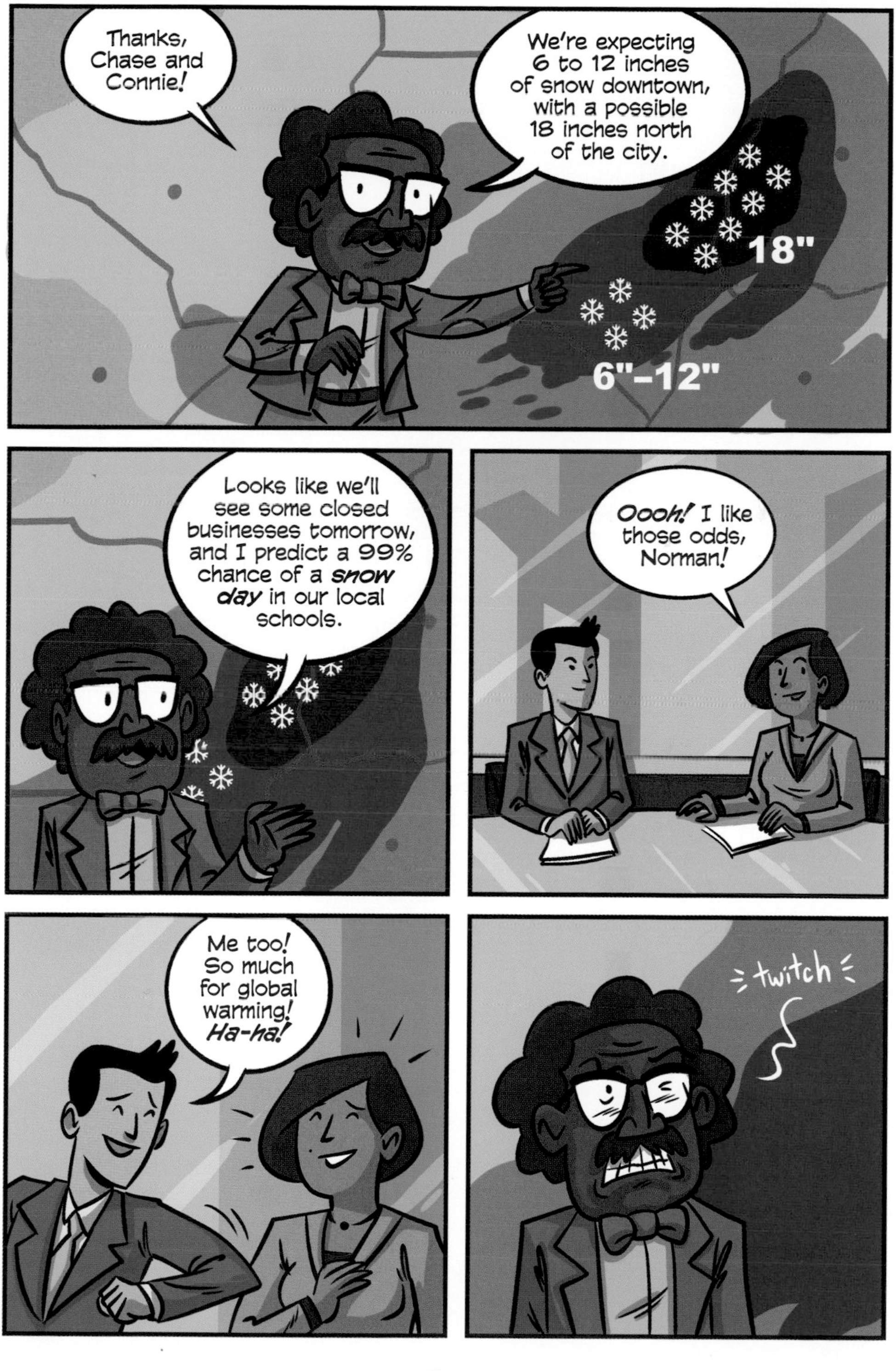

Thanks, Chase and Connie!
We're expecting 6 to 12 inches of snow downtown, with a possible 18 inches north of the city.
18"
6"–12"
Looks like we'll see some closed businesses tomorrow, and I predict a 99% chance of a *snow day* in our local schools.
Oooh! I like those odds, Norman!
Me too! So much for global warming! *Ha-ha!*
twitch

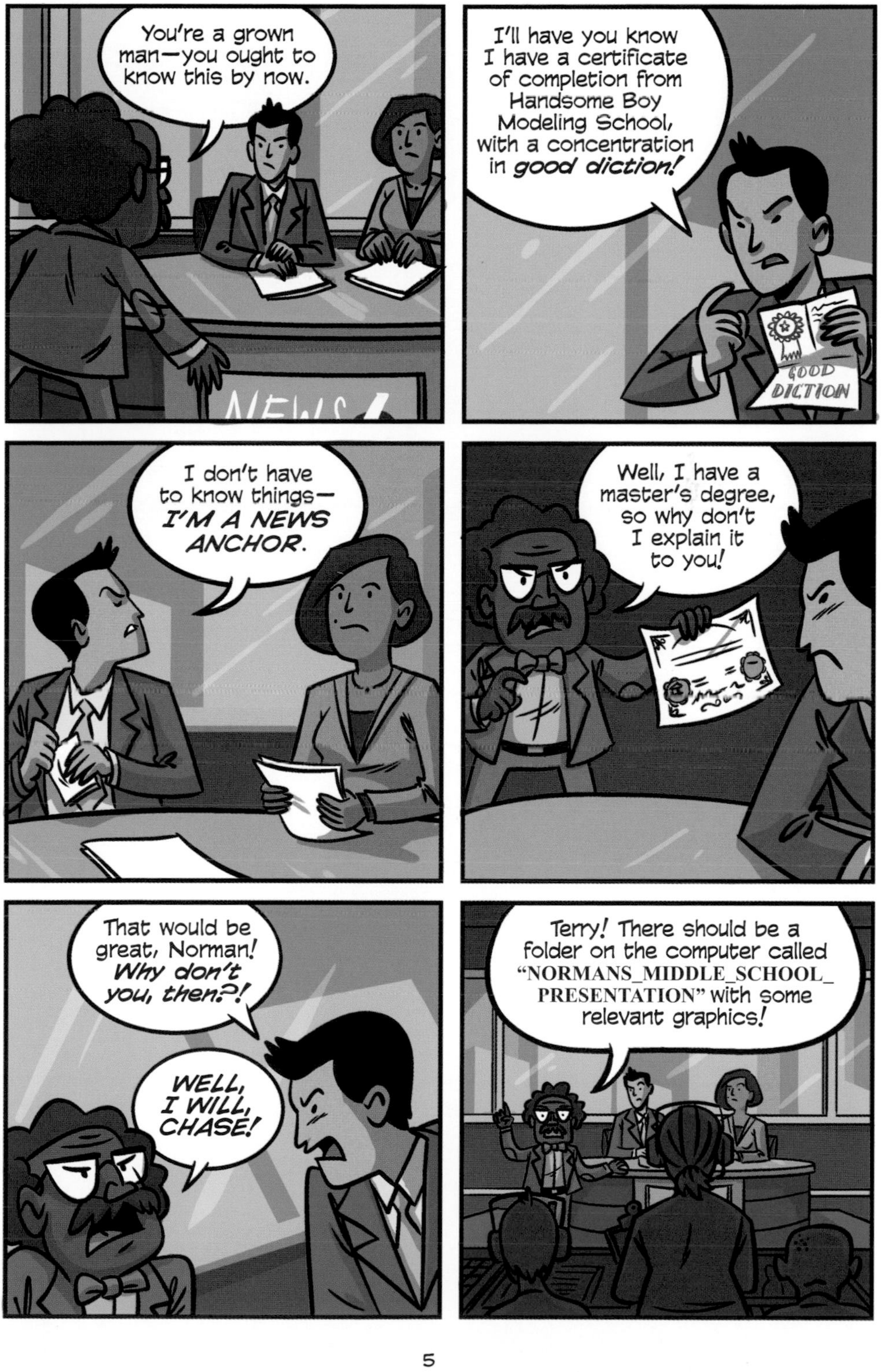
You're a grown man—you ought to know this by now.
NEWS
I'll have you know I have a certificate of completion from Handsome Boy Modeling School, with a concentration in *good diction!*
GOOD DICTION
I don't have to know things—*I'M A NEWS ANCHOR.*
Well, I have a master's degree, so why don't I explain it to you!
That would be great, Norman! *Why don't you, then?!*
WELL, I WILL, CHASE!
Terry! There should be a folder on the computer called "NORMANS_MIDDLE_SCHOOL_PRESENTATION" with some relevant graphics!

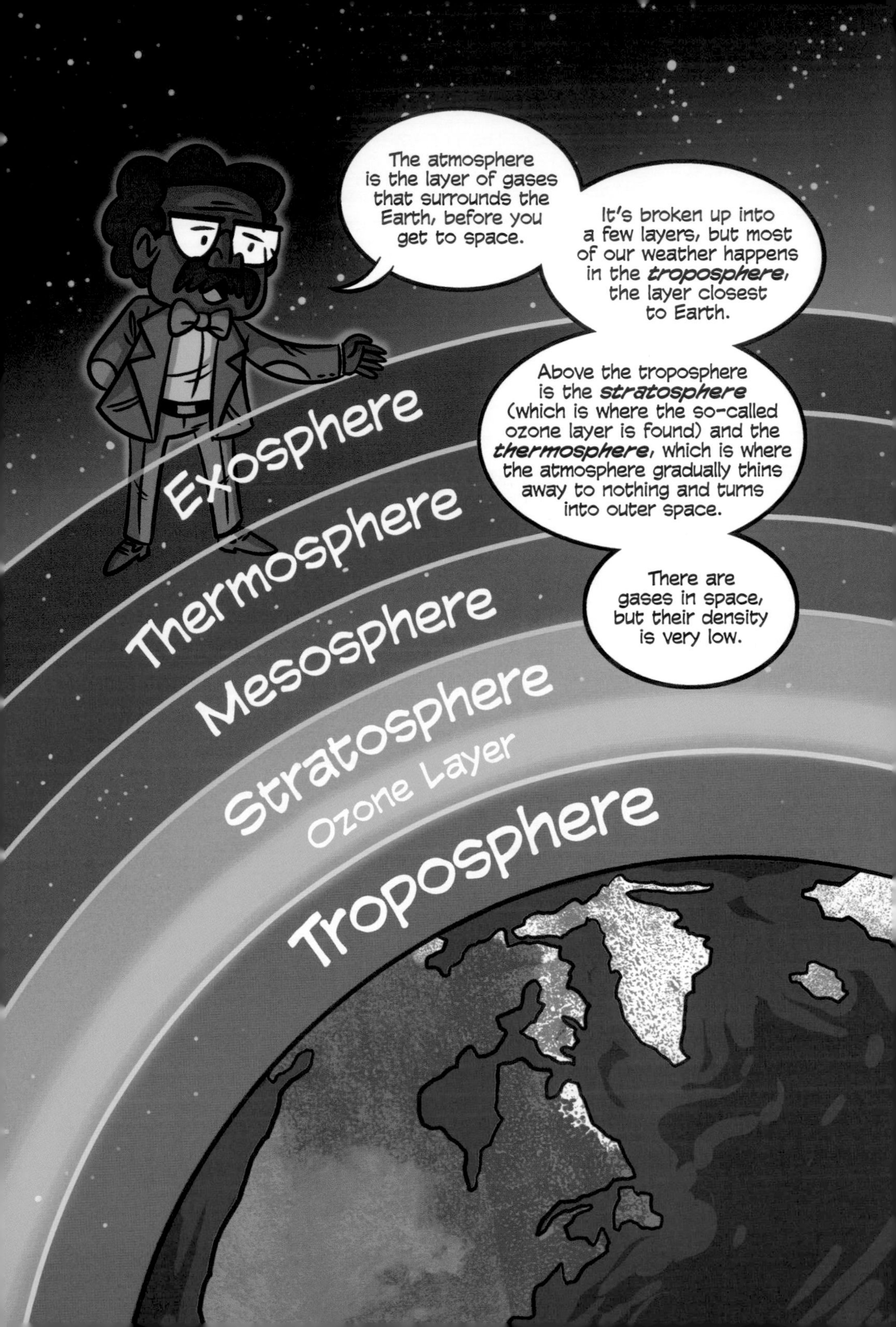
The atmosphere is the layer of gases that surrounds the Earth, before you get to space.
It's broken up into a few layers, but most of our weather happens in the *troposphere*, the layer closest to Earth.
Above the troposphere is the *stratosphere* (which is where the so-called ozone layer is found) and the *thermosphere*, which is where the atmosphere gradually thins away to nothing and turns into outer space.
There are gases in space, but their density is very low.
Exosphere
Thermosphere
Mesosphere
Stratosphere
Ozone Layer
Troposphere

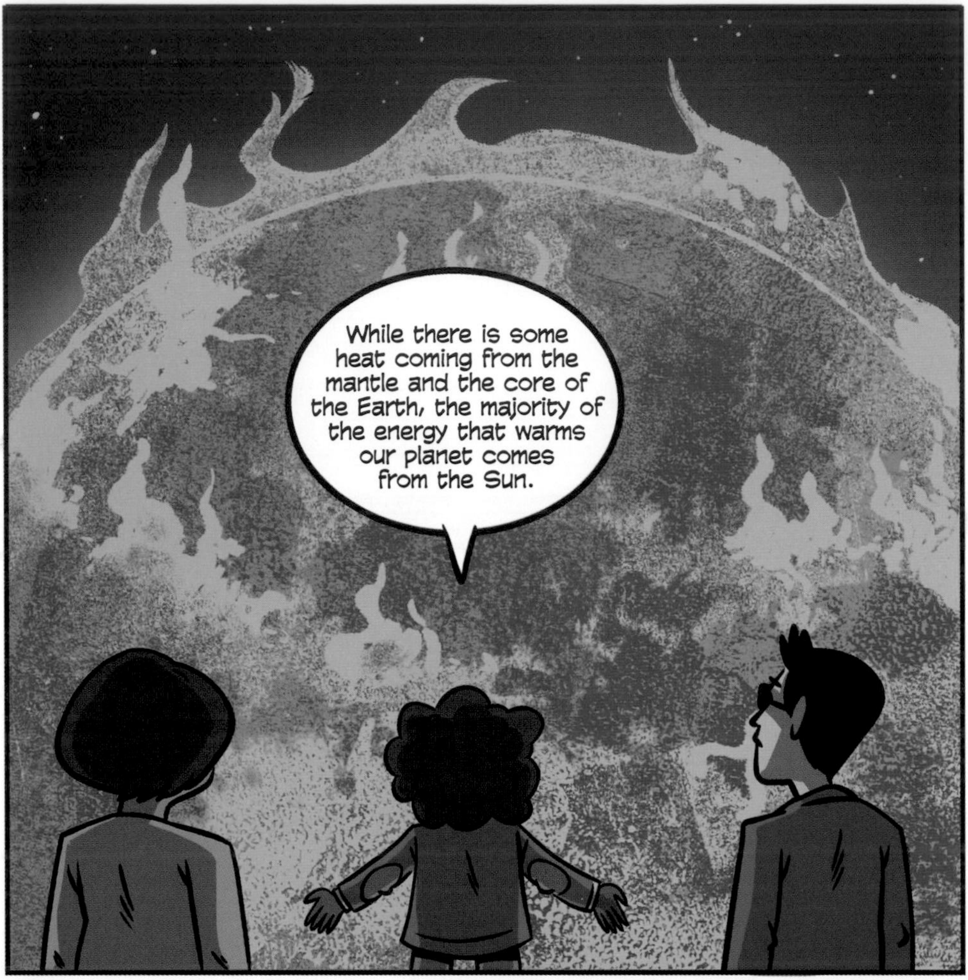
While there is some heat coming from the mantle and the core of the Earth, the majority of the energy that warms our planet comes from the Sun.

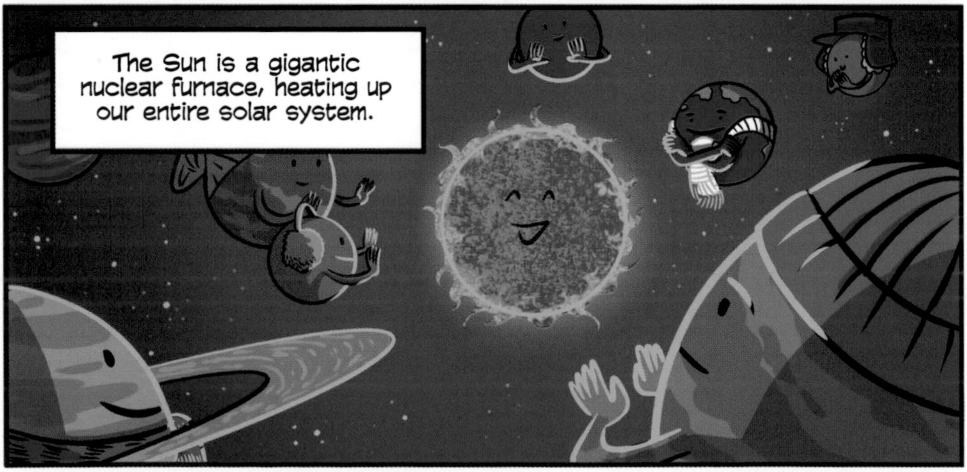
The Sun is a gigantic nuclear furnace, heating up our entire solar system.

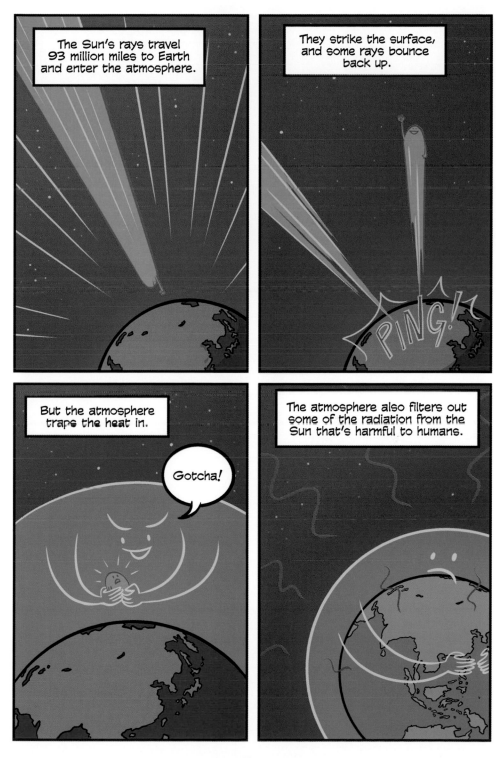

15

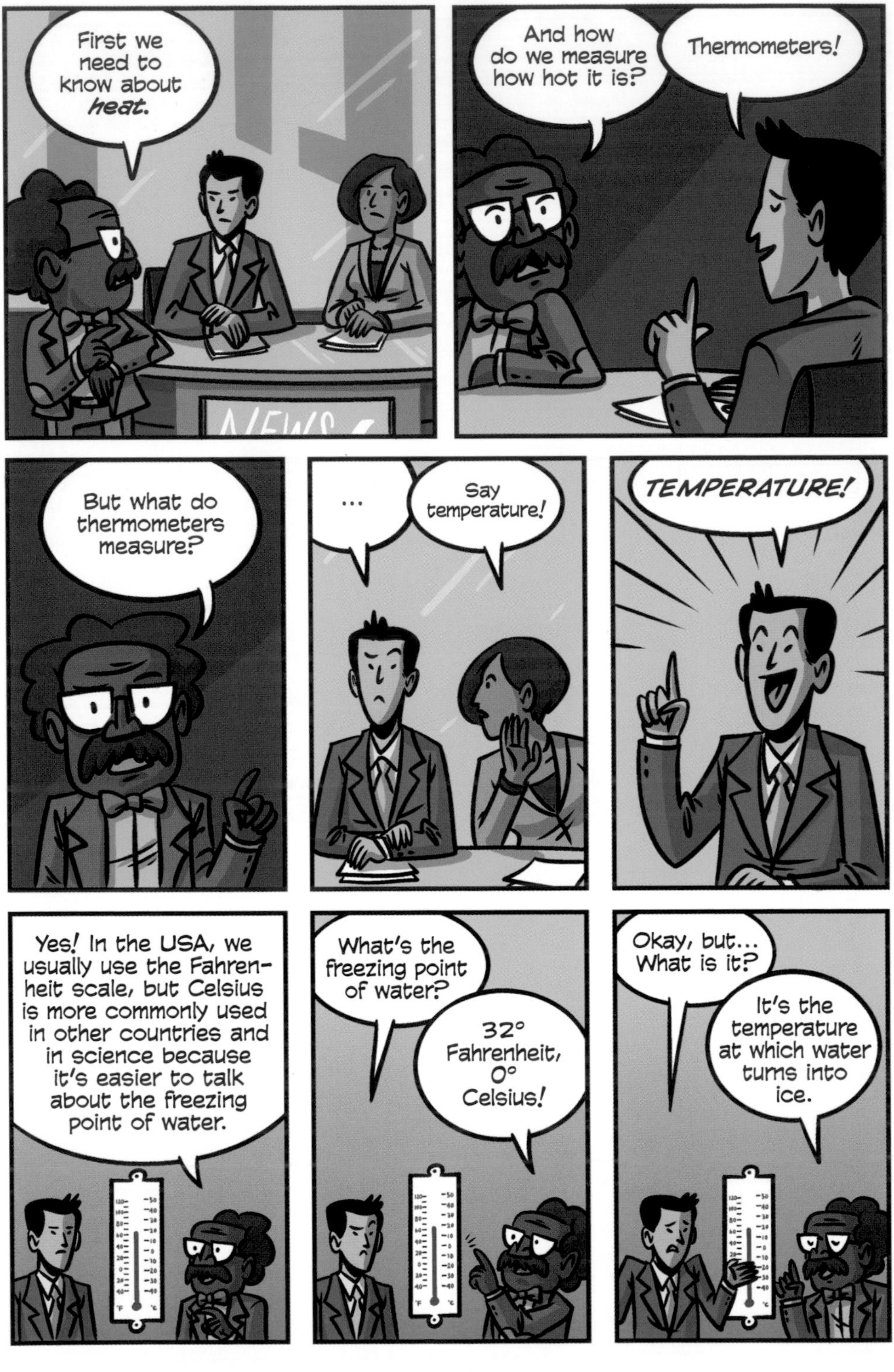
First we need to know about *heat*.
NEWS
And how do we measure how hot it is?
Thermometers!
But what do thermometers measure?
...
Say temperature!
TEMPERATURE!
Yes! In the USA, we usually use the Fahrenheit scale, but Celsius is more commonly used in other countries and in science because it's easier to talk about the freezing point of water.
What's the freezing point of water?
32° Fahrenheit, 0° Celsius!
Okay, but... What is it?
It's the temperature at which water turns into ice.

So hot air rises over cold air because it's less dense, and cold air sinks down.

When the hot air moves, cold air moves into the space it left.

And the cycle keeps going!

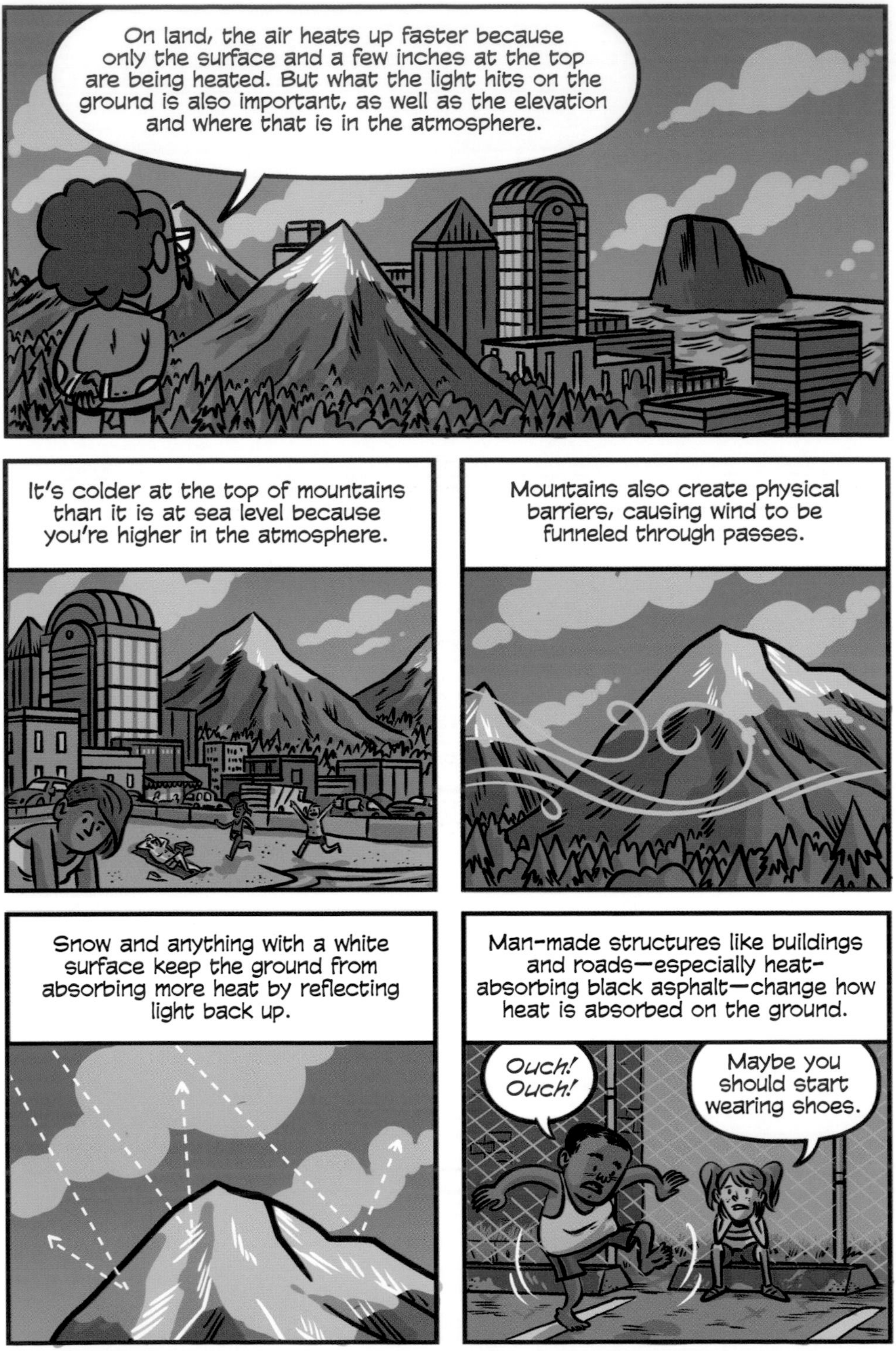

On land, the air heats up faster because only the surface and a few inches at the top are being heated. But what the light hits on the ground is also important, as well as the elevation and where that is in the atmosphere.
It's colder at the top of mountains than it is at sea level because you're higher in the atmosphere.
Mountains also create physical barriers, causing wind to be funneled through passes.
Snow and anything with a white surface keep the ground from absorbing more heat by reflecting light back up.
Man-made structures like buildings and roads—especially heat-absorbing black asphalt—change how heat is absorbed on the ground.
Ouch! Ouch!
Maybe you should start wearing shoes.

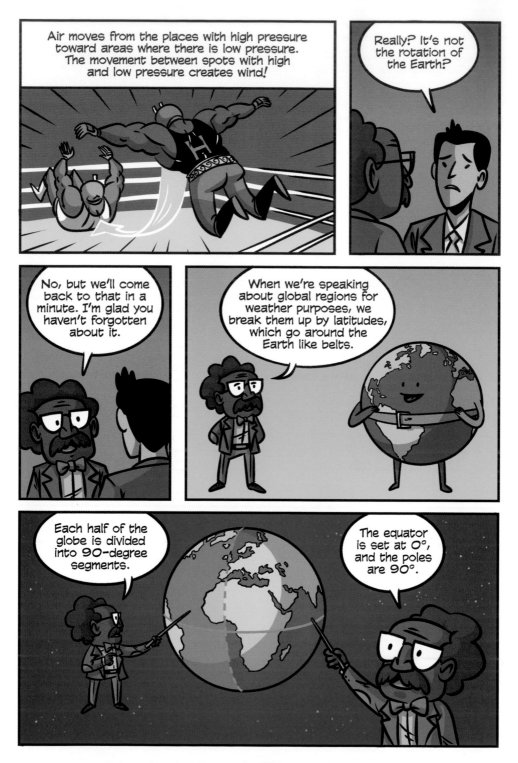

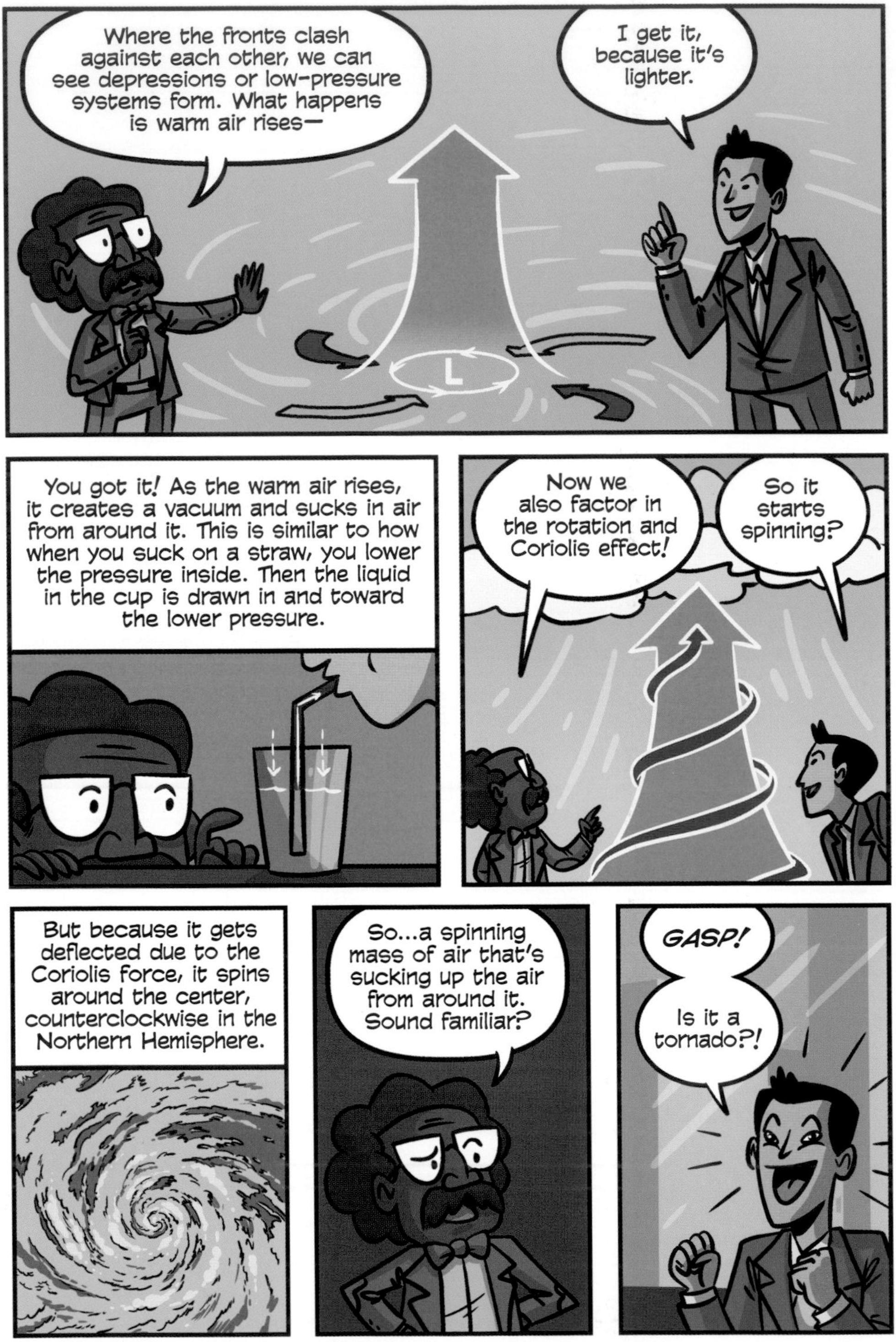
Where the fronts clash against each other, we can see depressions or low-pressure systems form. What happens is warm air rises—
I get it, because it's lighter.
L
You got it! As the warm air rises, it creates a vacuum and sucks in air from around it. This is similar to how when you suck on a straw, you lower the pressure inside. Then the liquid in the cup is drawn in and toward the lower pressure.
Now we also factor in the rotation and Coriolis effect!
So it starts spinning?
But because it gets deflected due to the Coriolis force, it spins around the center, counterclockwise in the Northern Hemisphere.
So...a spinning mass of air that's sucking up the air from around it. Sound familiar?
GASP!
Is it a tornado?!

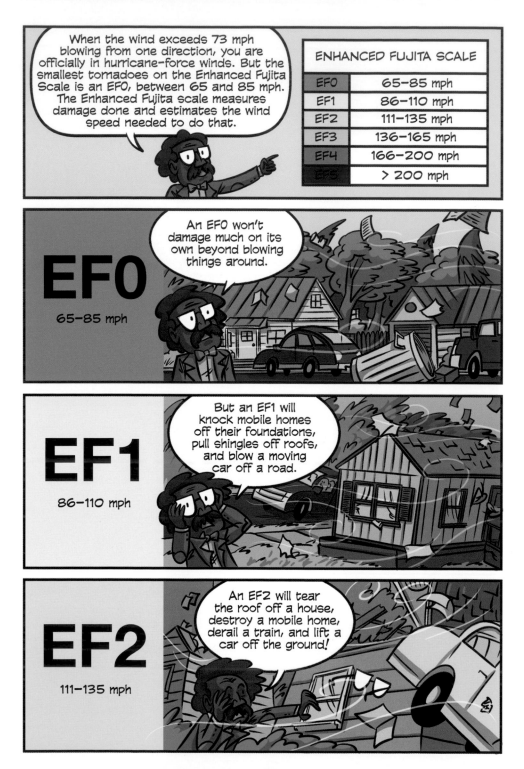

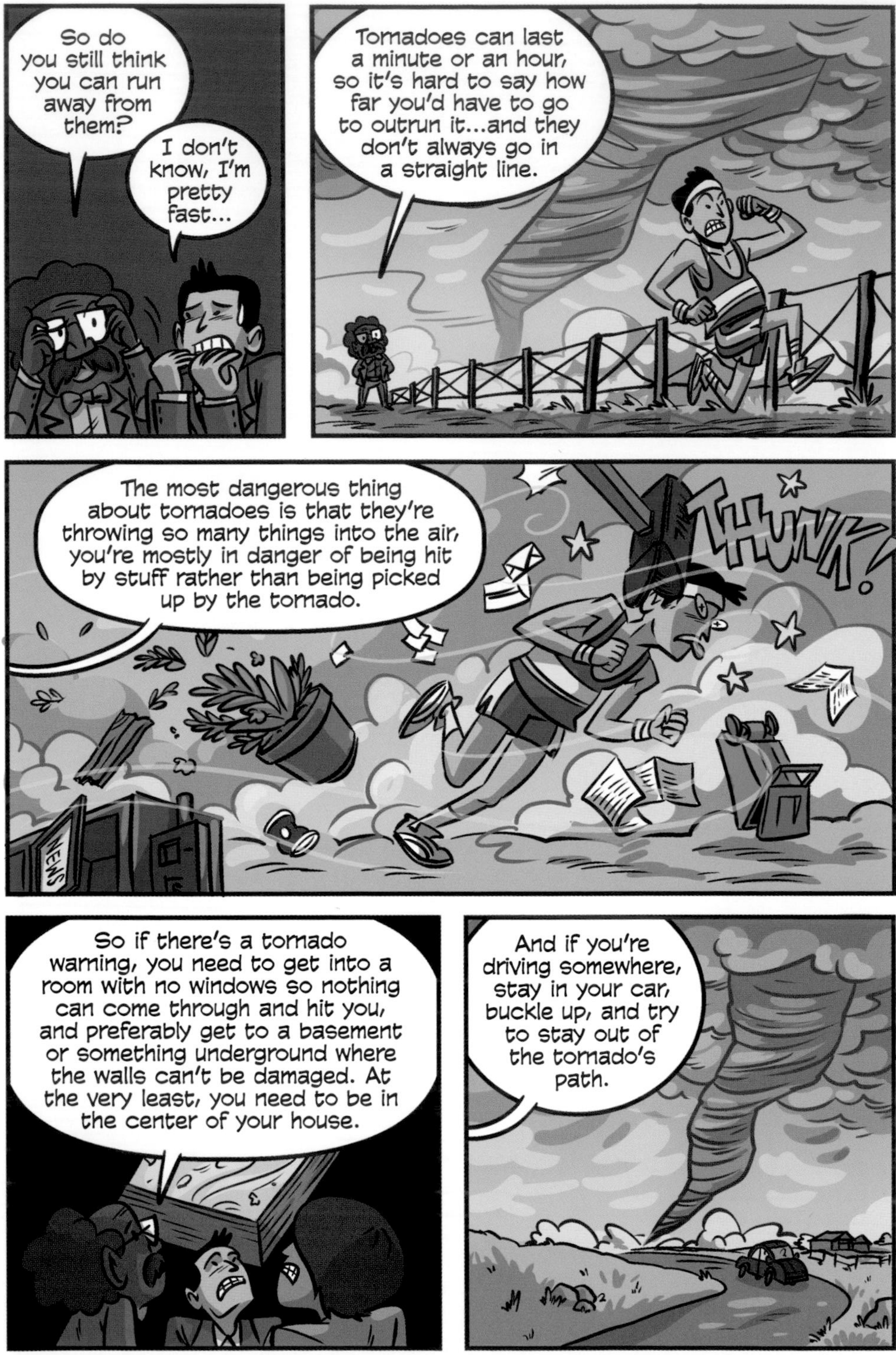

So do you still think you can run away from them?
I don't know, I'm pretty fast...
Tornadoes can last a minute or an hour, so it's hard to say how far you'd have to go to outrun it...and they don't always go in a straight line.
The most dangerous thing about tornadoes is that they're throwing so many things into the air, you're mostly in danger of being hit by stuff rather than being picked up by the tornado.
THUNK!
NEWS
So if there's a tornado warning, you need to get into a room with no windows so nothing can come through and hit you, and preferably get to a basement or something underground where the walls can't be damaged. At the very least, you need to be in the center of your house.
And if you're driving somewhere, stay in your car, buckle up, and try to stay out of the tornado's path.

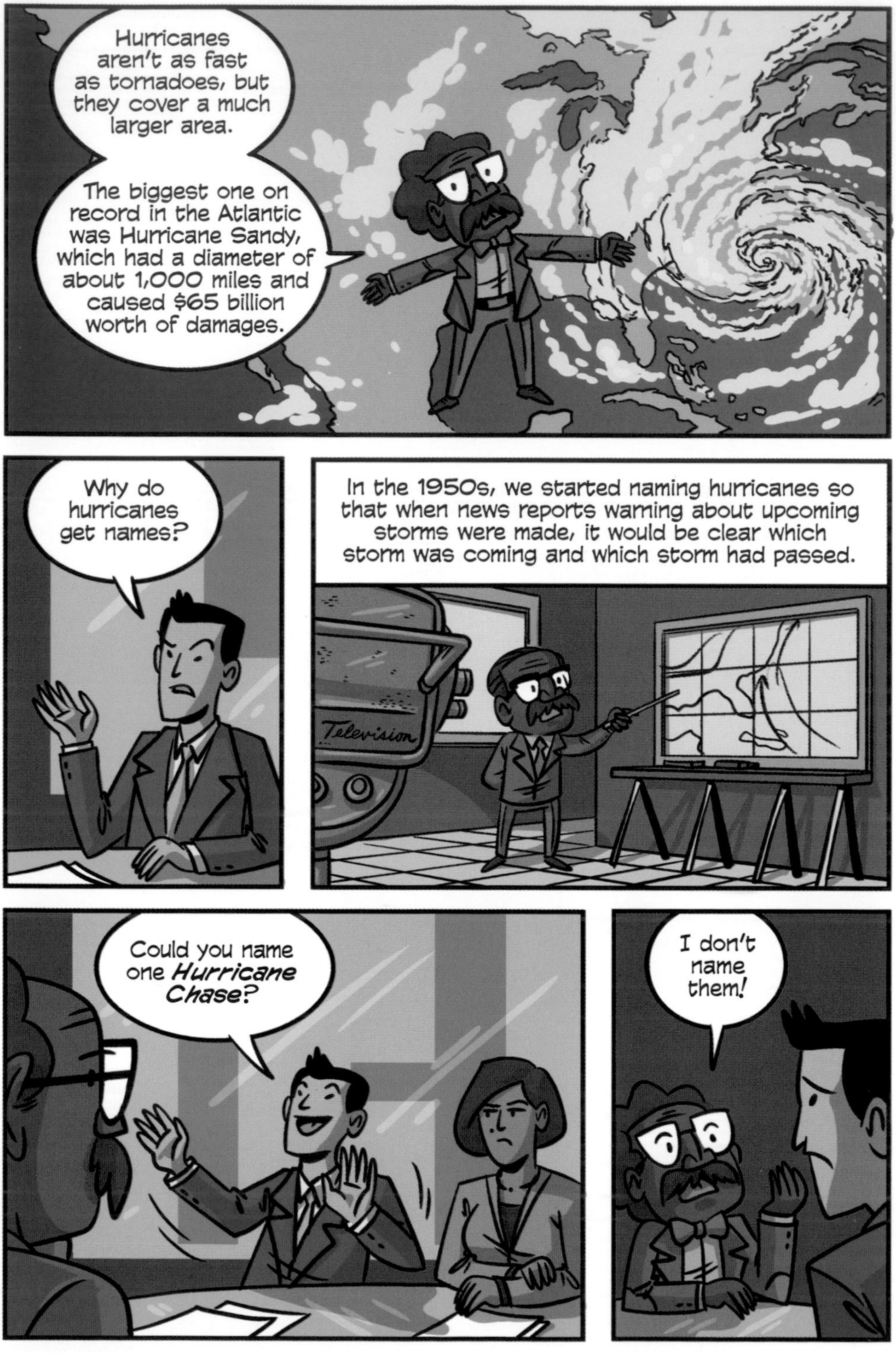

Hurricanes aren't as fast as tornadoes, but they cover a much larger area.
The biggest one on record in the Atlantic was Hurricane Sandy, which had a diameter of about 1,000 miles and caused $65 billion worth of damages.
Why do hurricanes get names?
In the 1950s, we started naming hurricanes so that when news reports warning about upcoming storms were made, it would be clear which storm was coming and which storm had passed.
Television
Could you name one *Hurricane Chase*?
I don't name them!

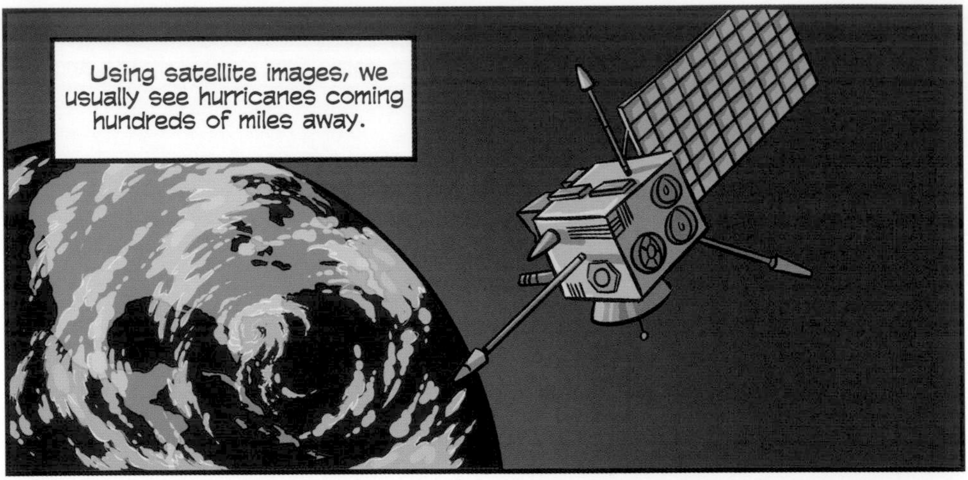
Using satellite images, we usually see hurricanes coming hundreds of miles away.

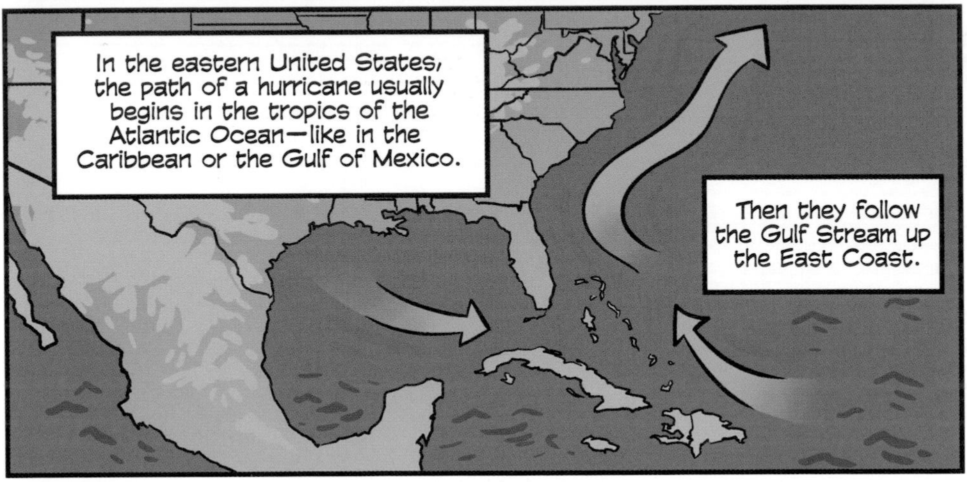
In the eastern United States, the path of a hurricane usually begins in the tropics of the Atlantic Ocean—like in the Caribbean or the Gulf of Mexico.
Then they follow the Gulf Stream up the East Coast.

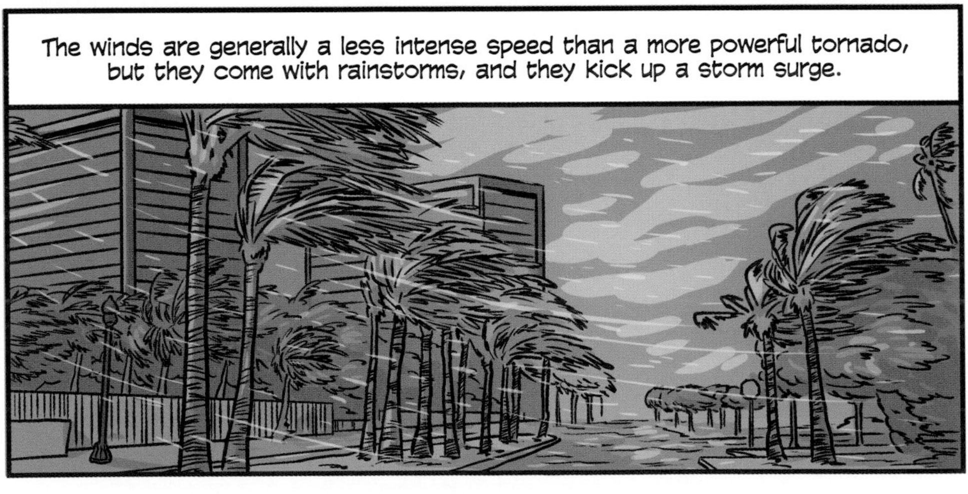
The winds are generally a less intense speed than a more powerful tornado, but they come with rainstorms, and they kick up a storm surge.

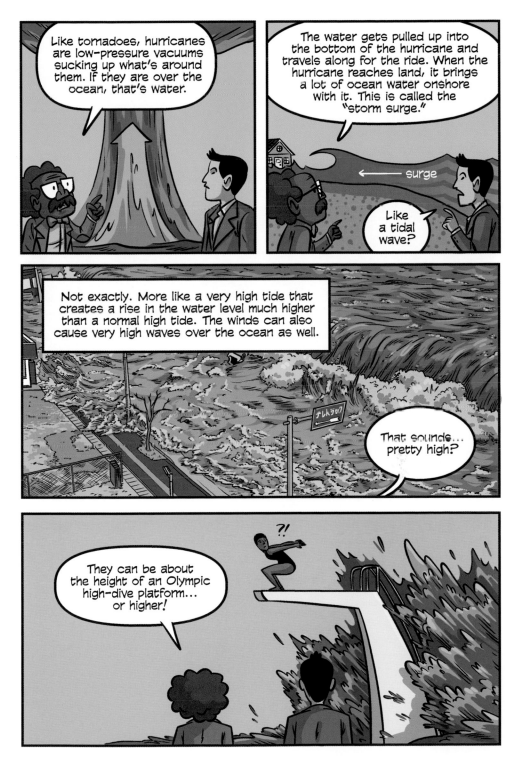

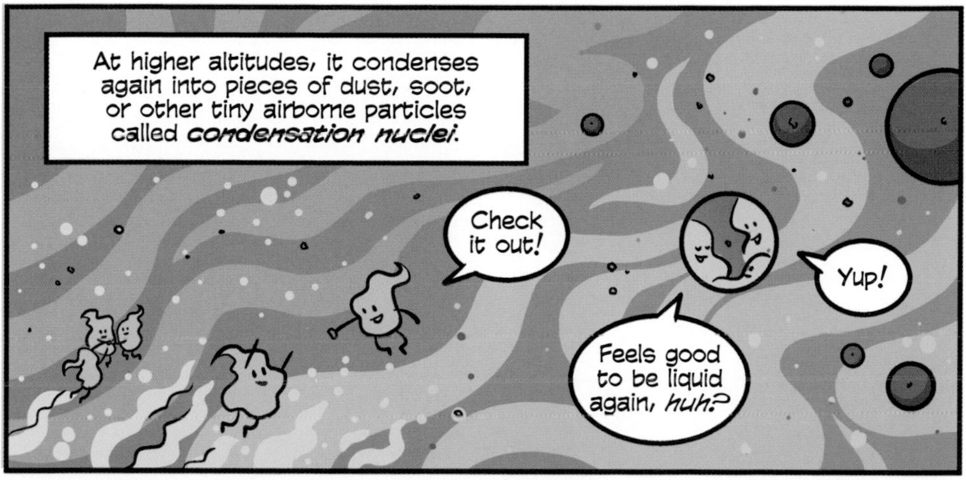
At higher altitudes, it condenses again into pieces of dust, soot, or other tiny airborne particles called *condensation nuclei*.
Check it out!
Feels good to be liquid again, *huh?*
Yup!

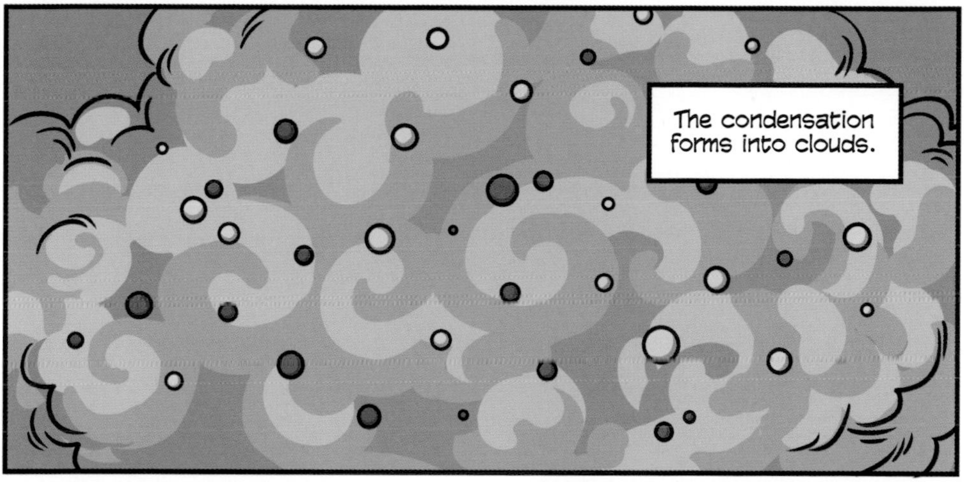
The condensation forms into clouds.

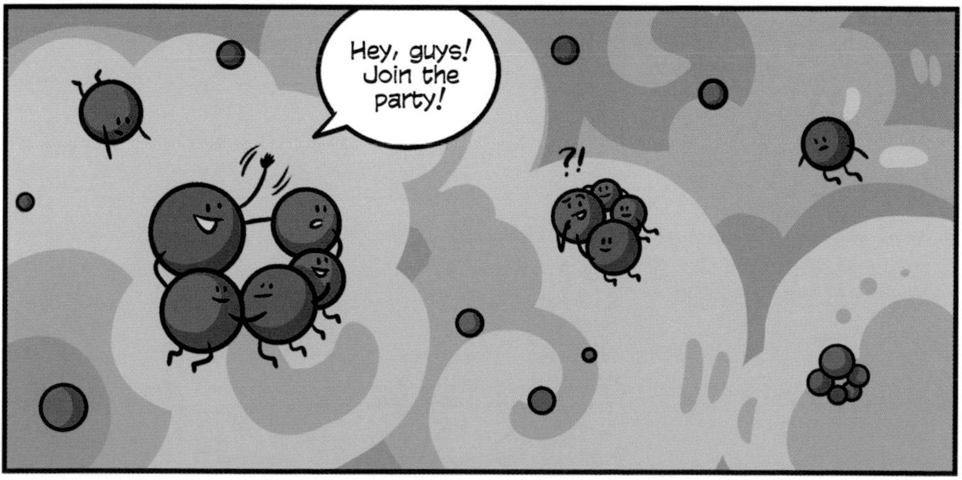
Hey, guys! Join the party!
?!

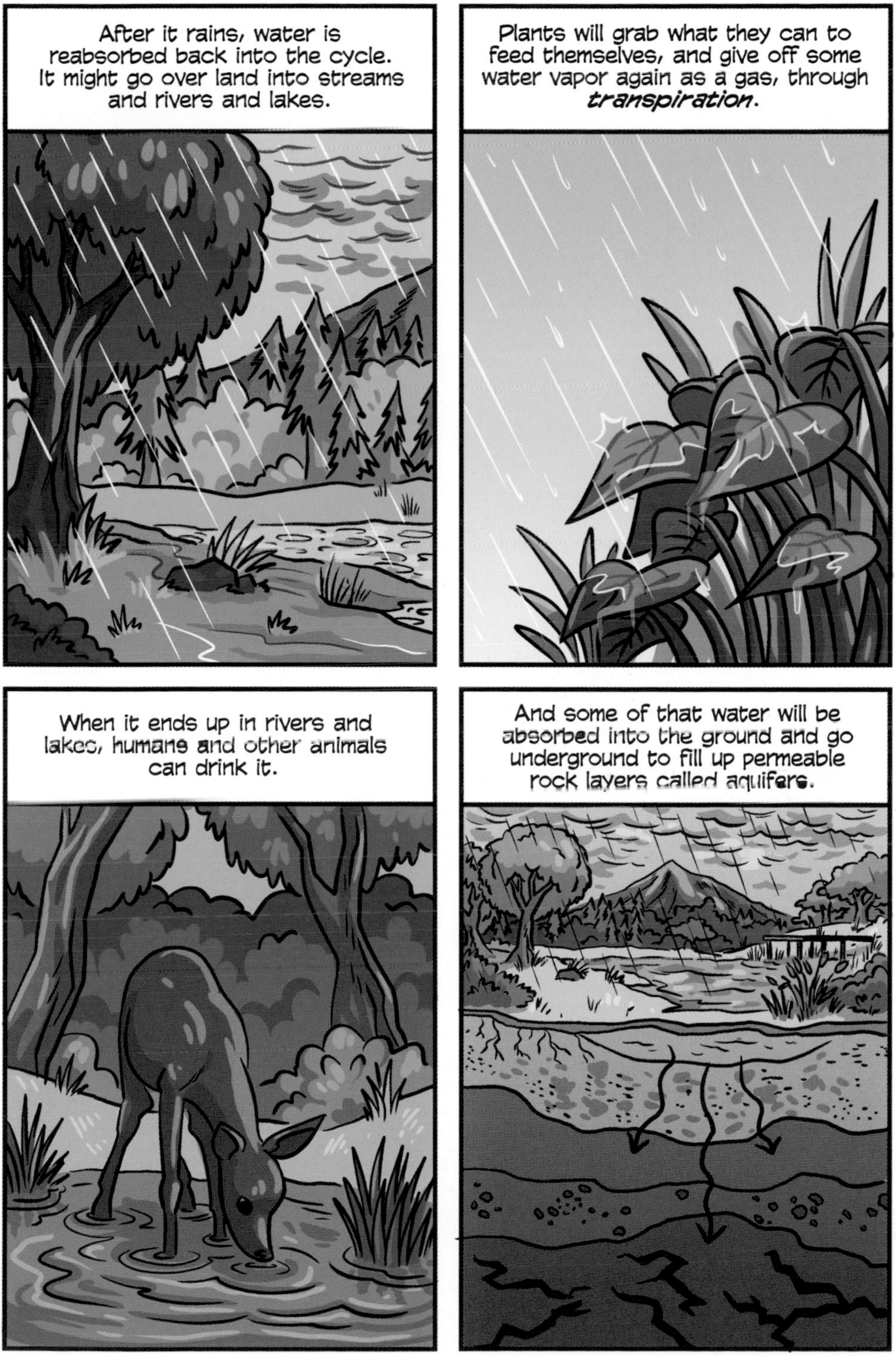
After it rains, water is reabsorbed back into the cycle. It might go over land into streams and rivers and lakes.
Plants will grab what they can to feed themselves, and give off some water vapor again as a gas, through ***transpiration***.
When it ends up in rivers and lakes, humans and other animals can drink it.
And some of that water will be absorbed into the ground and go underground to fill up permeable rock layers called aquifers.

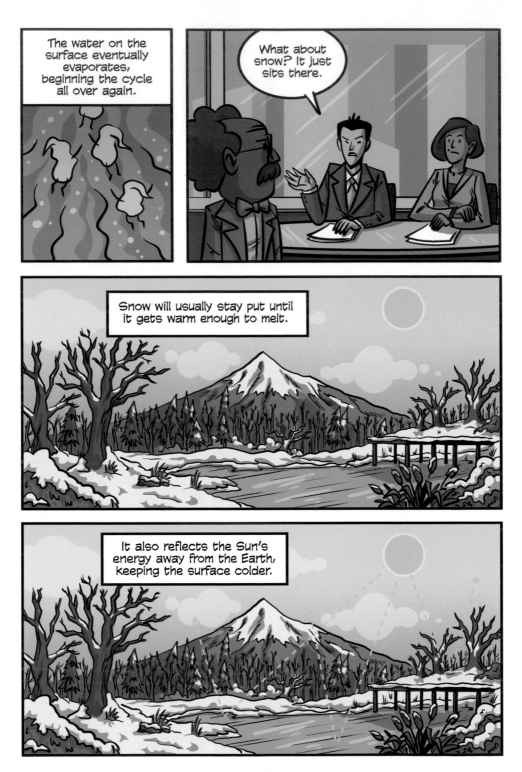

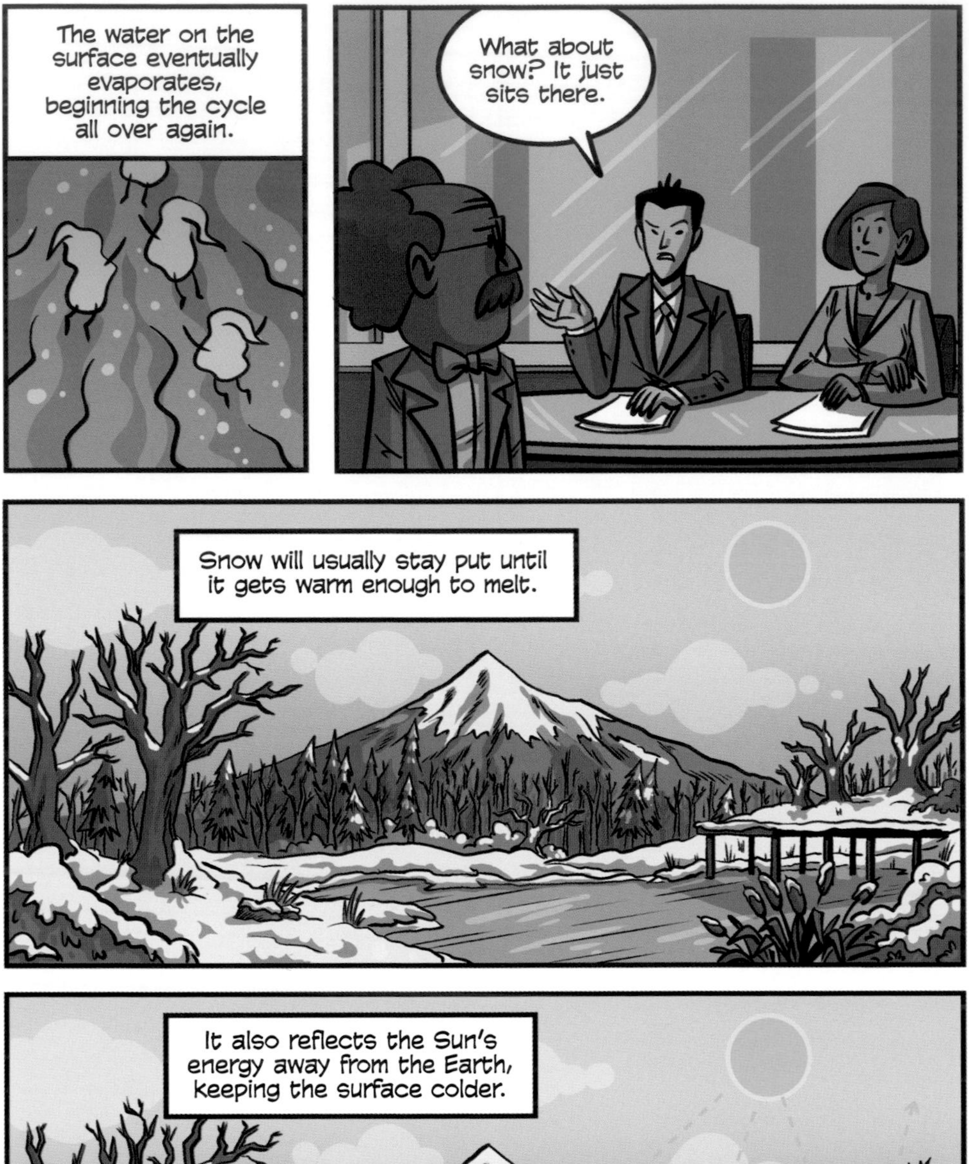
The water on the surface eventually evaporates, beginning the cycle all over again.
What about snow? It just sits there.
Snow will usually stay put until it gets warm enough to melt.
It also reflects the Sun's energy away from the Earth, keeping the surface colder.

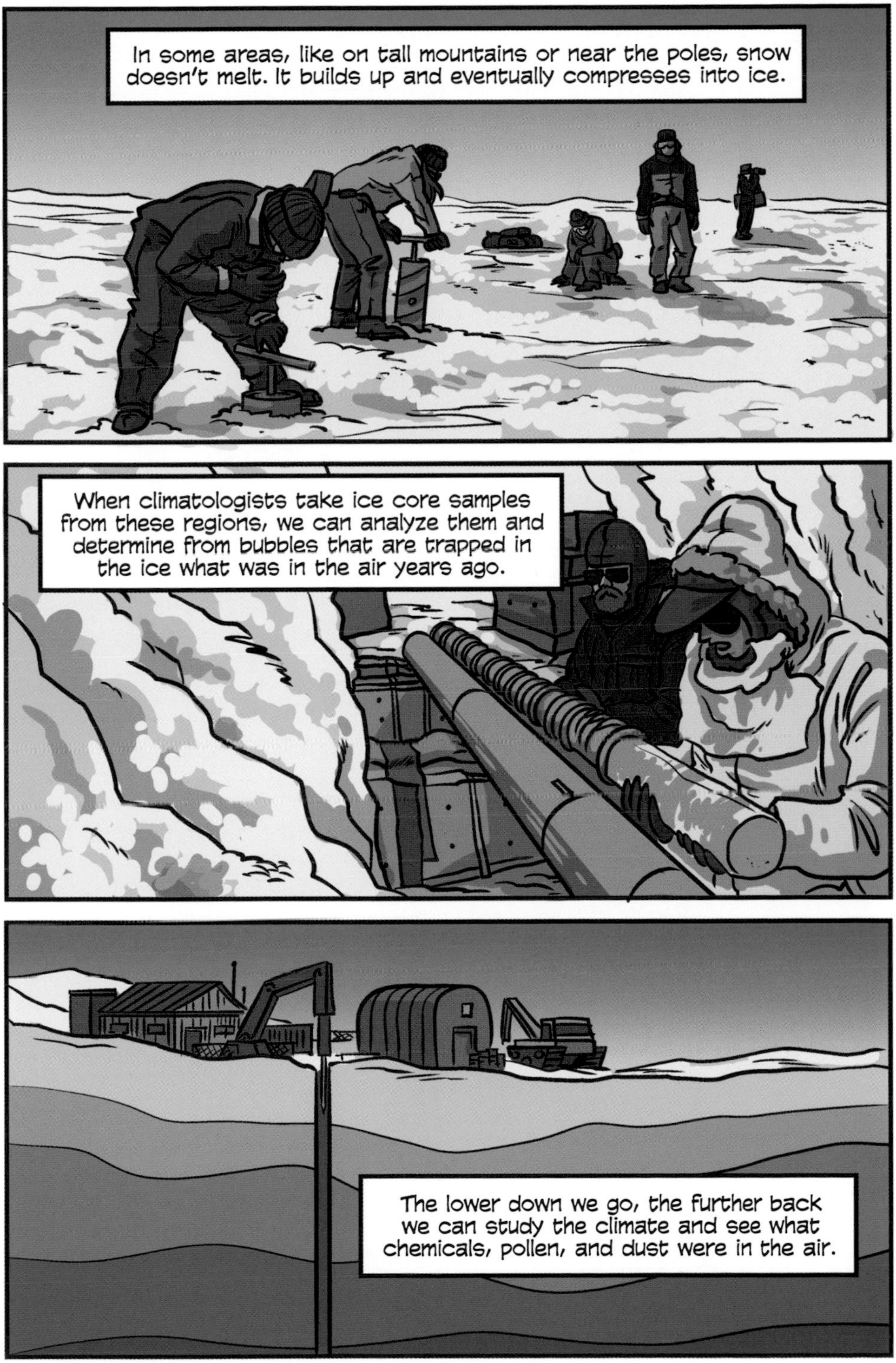
In some areas, like on tall mountains or near the poles, snow doesn't melt. It builds up and eventually compresses into ice.
When climatologists take ice core samples from these regions, we can analyze them and determine from bubbles that are trapped in the ice what was in the air years ago.
The lower down we go, the further back we can study the climate and see what chemicals, pollen, and dust were in the air.

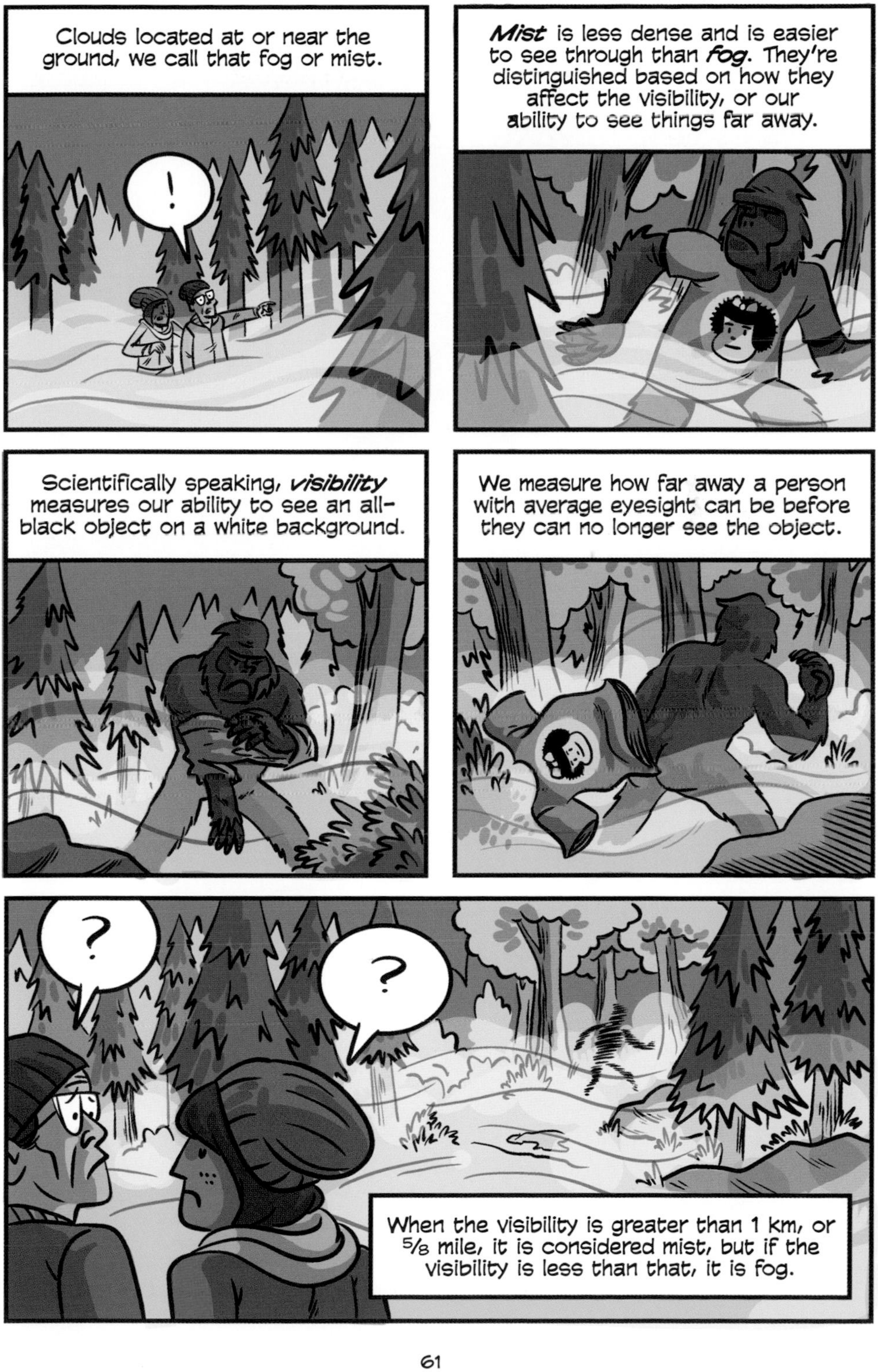

Clouds located at or near the ground, we call that fog or mist.
!
Mist is less dense and is easier to see through than *fog*. They're distinguished based on how they affect the visibility, or our ability to see things far away.
Scientifically speaking, *visibility* measures our ability to see an all-black object on a white background.
We measure how far away a person with average eyesight can be before they can no longer see the object.
?
?
When the visibility is greater than 1 km, or 5/8 mile, it is considered mist, but if the visibility is less than that, it is fog.

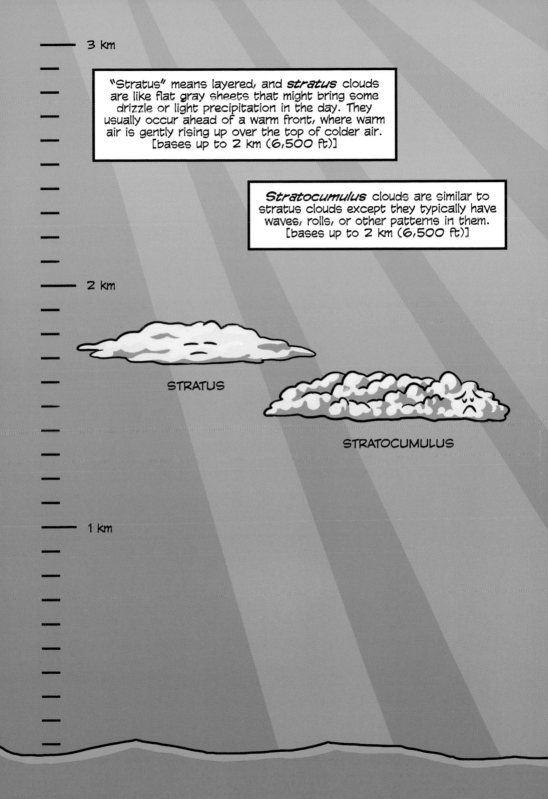

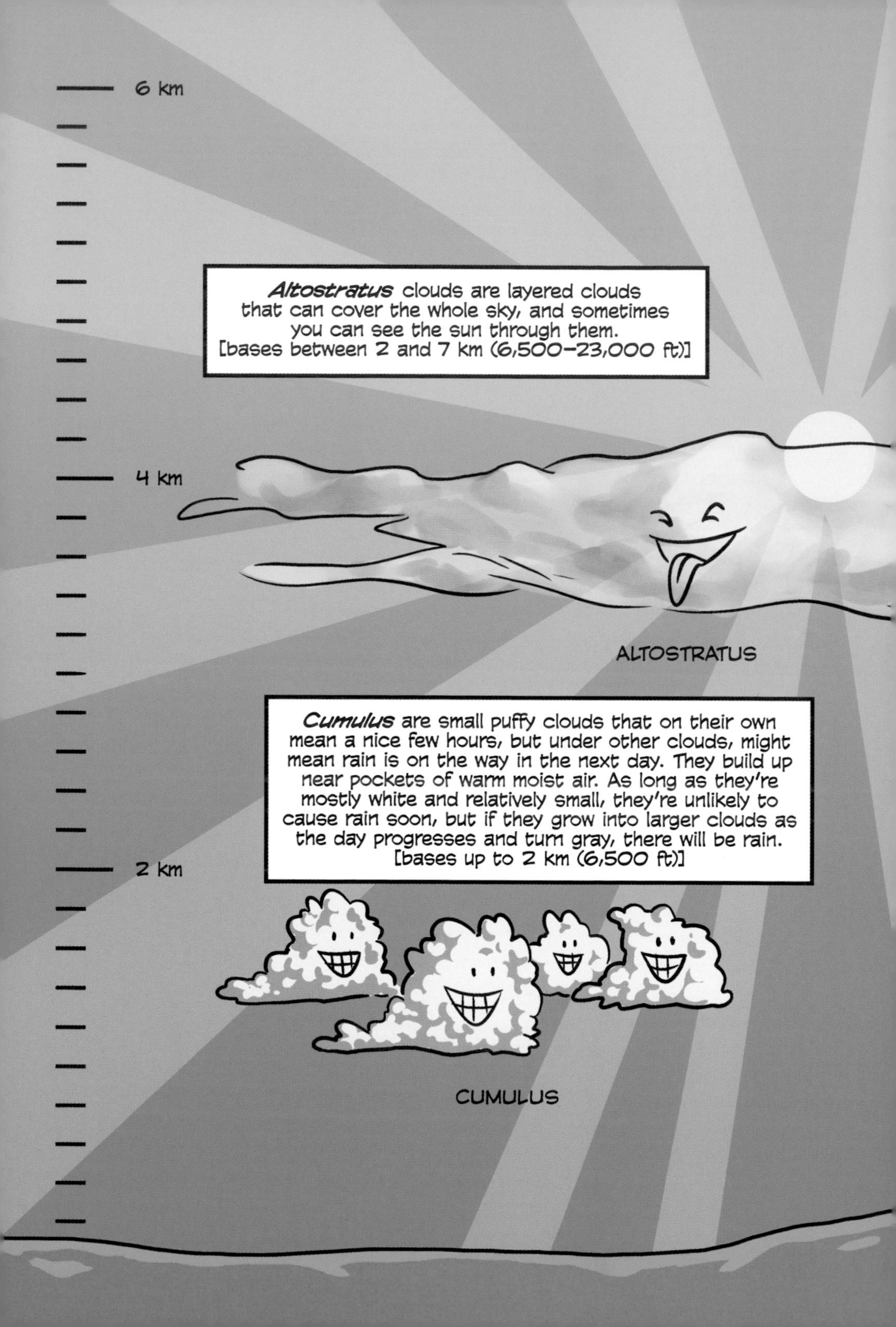
6 km
Altostratus clouds are layered clouds that can cover the whole sky, and sometimes you can see the sun through them. [bases between 2 and 7 km (6,500–23,000 ft)]
4 km
ALTOSTRATUS
Cumulus are small puffy clouds that on their own mean a nice few hours, but under other clouds, might mean rain is on the way in the next day. They build up near pockets of warm moist air. As long as they're mostly white and relatively small, they're unlikely to cause rain soon, but if they grow into larger clouds as the day progresses and turn gray, there will be rain. [bases up to 2 km (6,500 ft)]
2 km
CUMULUS

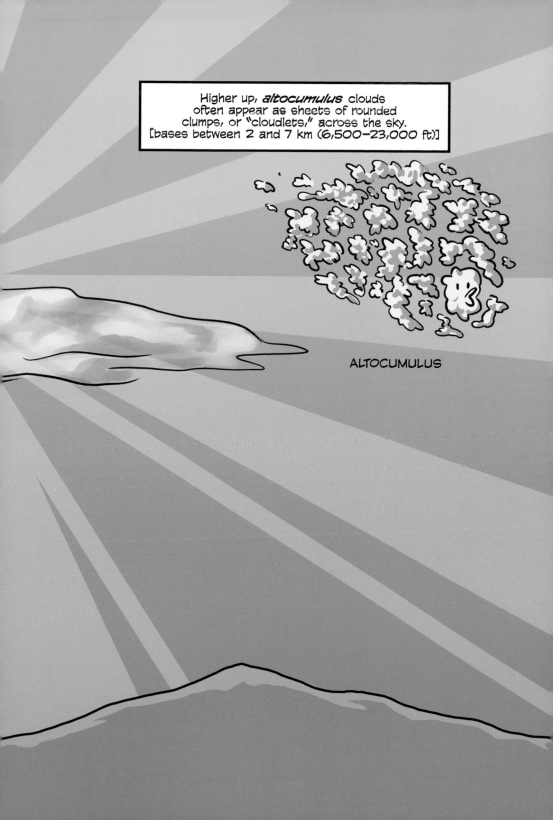

Higher up, *altocumulus* clouds often appear as sheets of rounded clumps, or "cloudlets," across the sky. [bases between 2 and 7 km (6,500–23,000 ft)]

ALTOCUMULUS

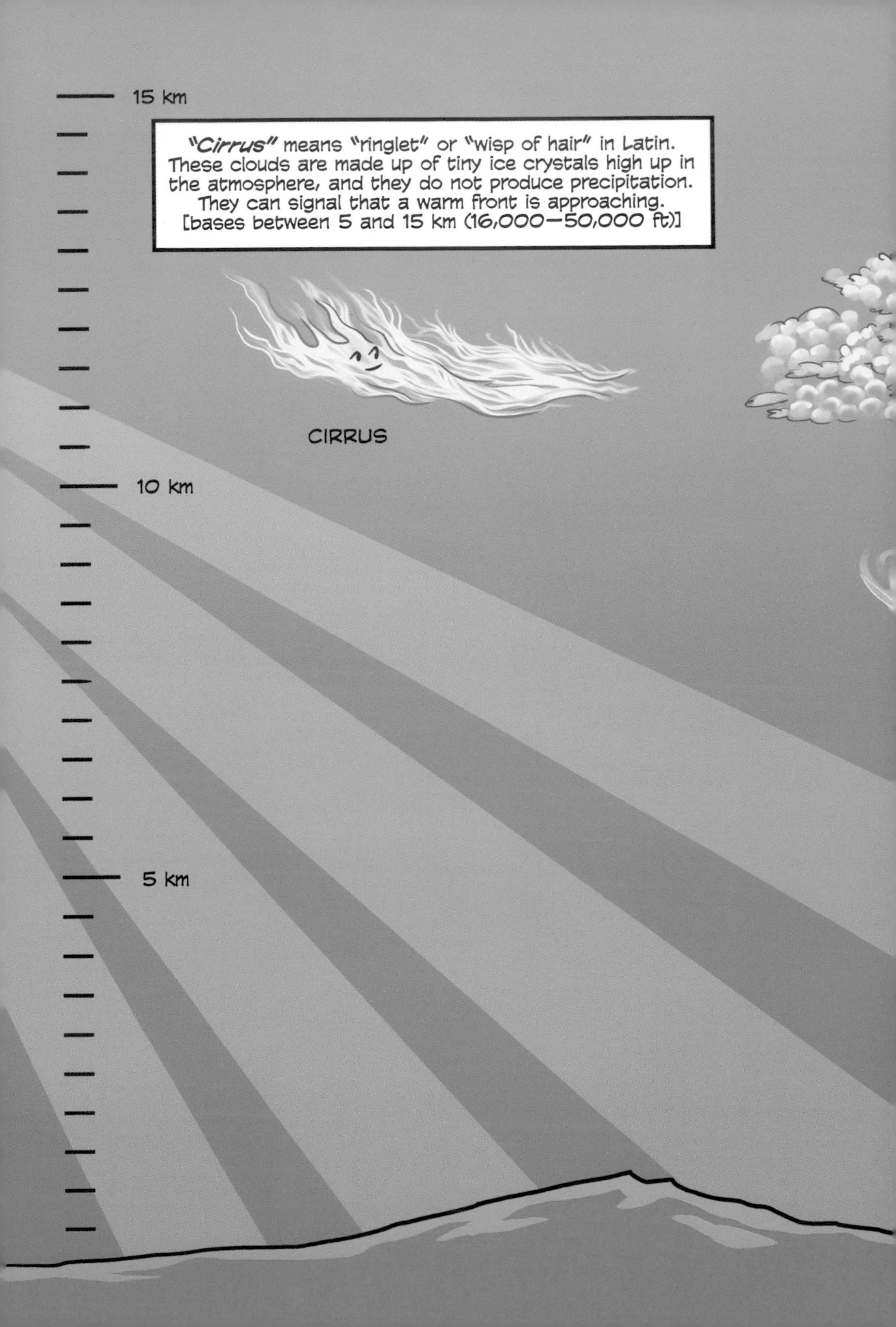
15 km
"Cirrus" means "ringlet" or "wisp of hair" in Latin. These clouds are made up of tiny ice crystals high up in the atmosphere, and they do not produce precipitation. They can signal that a warm front is approaching. [bases between 5 and 15 km (16,000—50,000 ft)]
CIRRUS
10 km
5 km

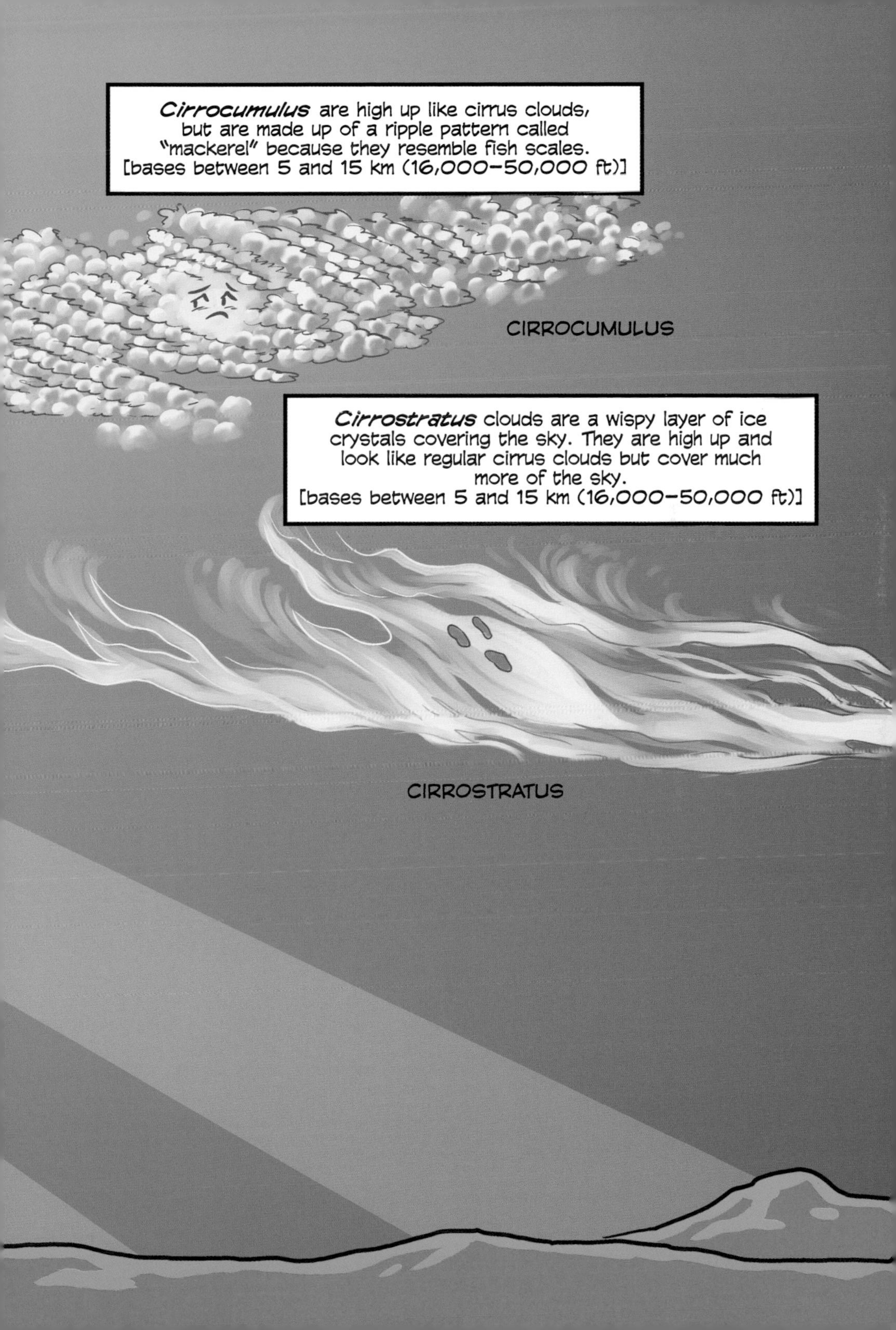

Cirrocumulus are high up like cirrus clouds, but are made up of a ripple pattern called "mackerel" because they resemble fish scales. [bases between 5 and 15 km (16,000–50,000 ft)]
CIRROCUMULUS
Cirrostratus clouds are a wispy layer of ice crystals covering the sky. They are high up and look like regular cirrus clouds but cover much more of the sky. [bases between 5 and 15 km (16,000–50,000 ft)]
CIRROSTRATUS

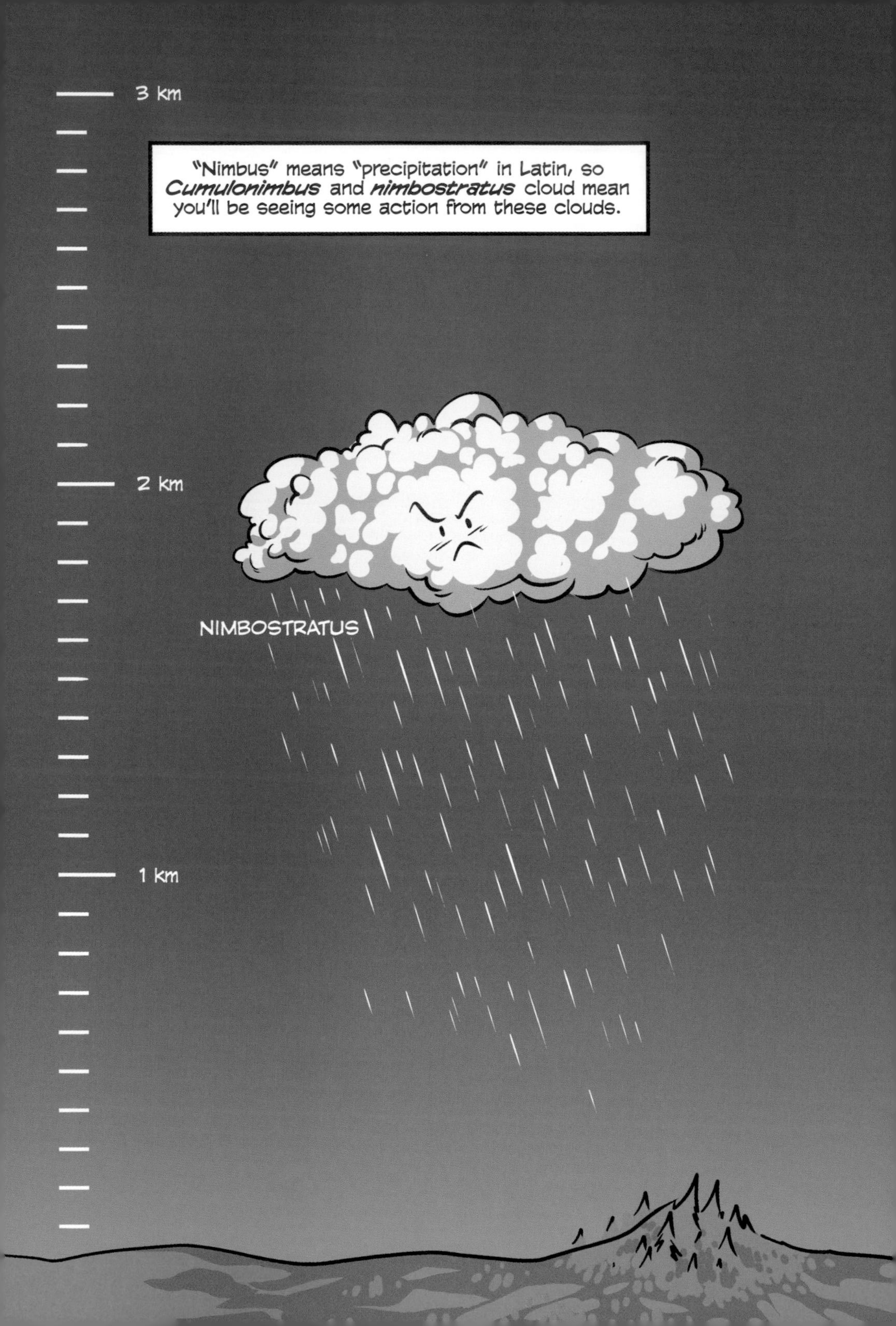
3 km
"Nimbus" means "precipitation" in Latin, so *Cumulonimbus* and *nimbostratus* cloud mean you'll be seeing some action from these clouds.
2 km
NIMBOSTRATUS
1 km

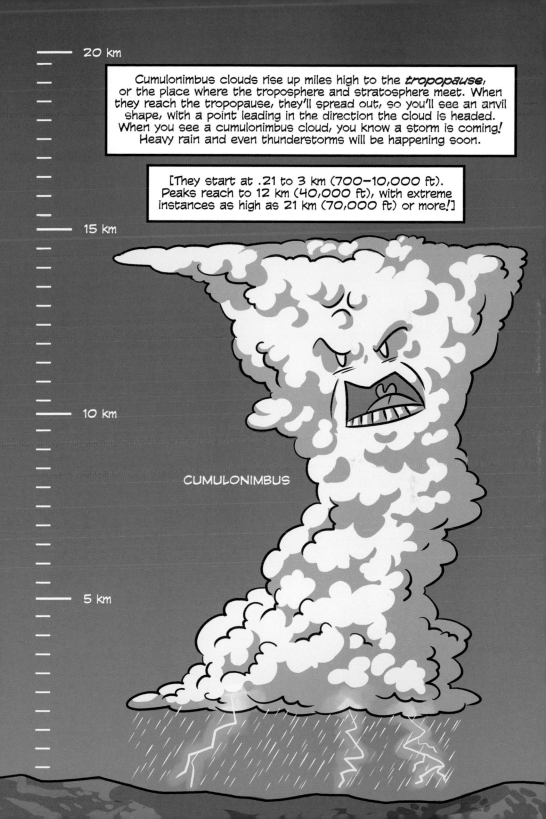

20 km

Cumulonimbus clouds rise up miles high to the *tropopause*, or the place where the troposphere and stratosphere meet. When they reach the tropopause, they'll spread out, so you'll see an anvil shape, with a point leading in the direction the cloud is headed. When you see a cumulonimbus cloud, you know a storm is coming! Heavy rain and even thunderstorms will be happening soon.

[They start at .21 to 3 km (700–10,000 ft). Peaks reach to 12 km (40,000 ft), with extreme instances as high as 21 km (70,000 ft) or more!]

15 km

10 km

CUMULONIMBUS

5 km

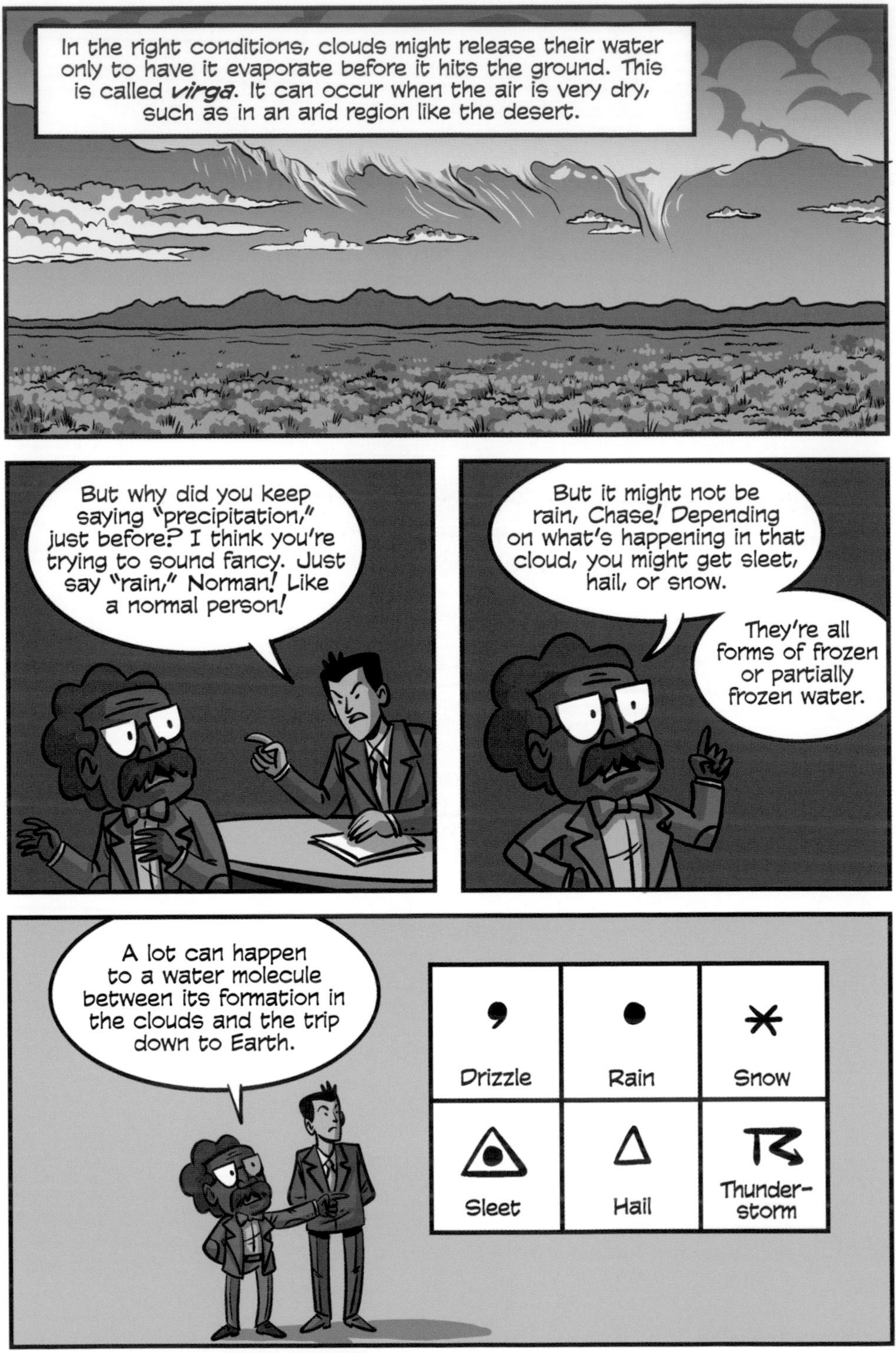
In the right conditions, clouds might release their water only to have it evaporate before it hits the ground. This is called *virga*. It can occur when the air is very dry, such as in an arid region like the desert.
But why did you keep saying "precipitation," just before? I think you're trying to sound fancy. Just say "rain," Norman! Like a normal person!
But it might not be rain, Chase! Depending on what's happening in that cloud, you might get sleet, hail, or snow.
They're all forms of frozen or partially frozen water.
A lot can happen to a water molecule between its formation in the clouds and the trip down to Earth.
Drizzle
Rain
Snow
Sleet
Hail
Thunder-storm

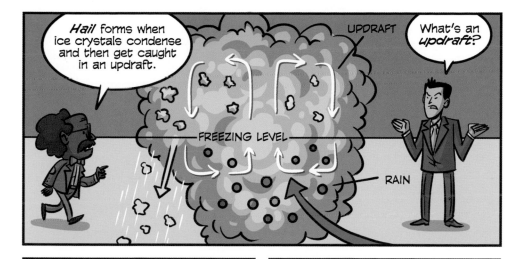

It's a warmer part of air within the cloud that pushes precipitation back upward. So hail goes through the place where ice is condensing again and grows bigger each time it passes through.

Sometimes hail particles rise and fall many times in updrafts and downdrafts, and then it can get quite large before it gets heavy enough to fall.

Usually we talk about the size of hail as being pea-sized or golf-ball-sized, but sometimes hail can get up to baseball- or grapefruit-sized pieces.

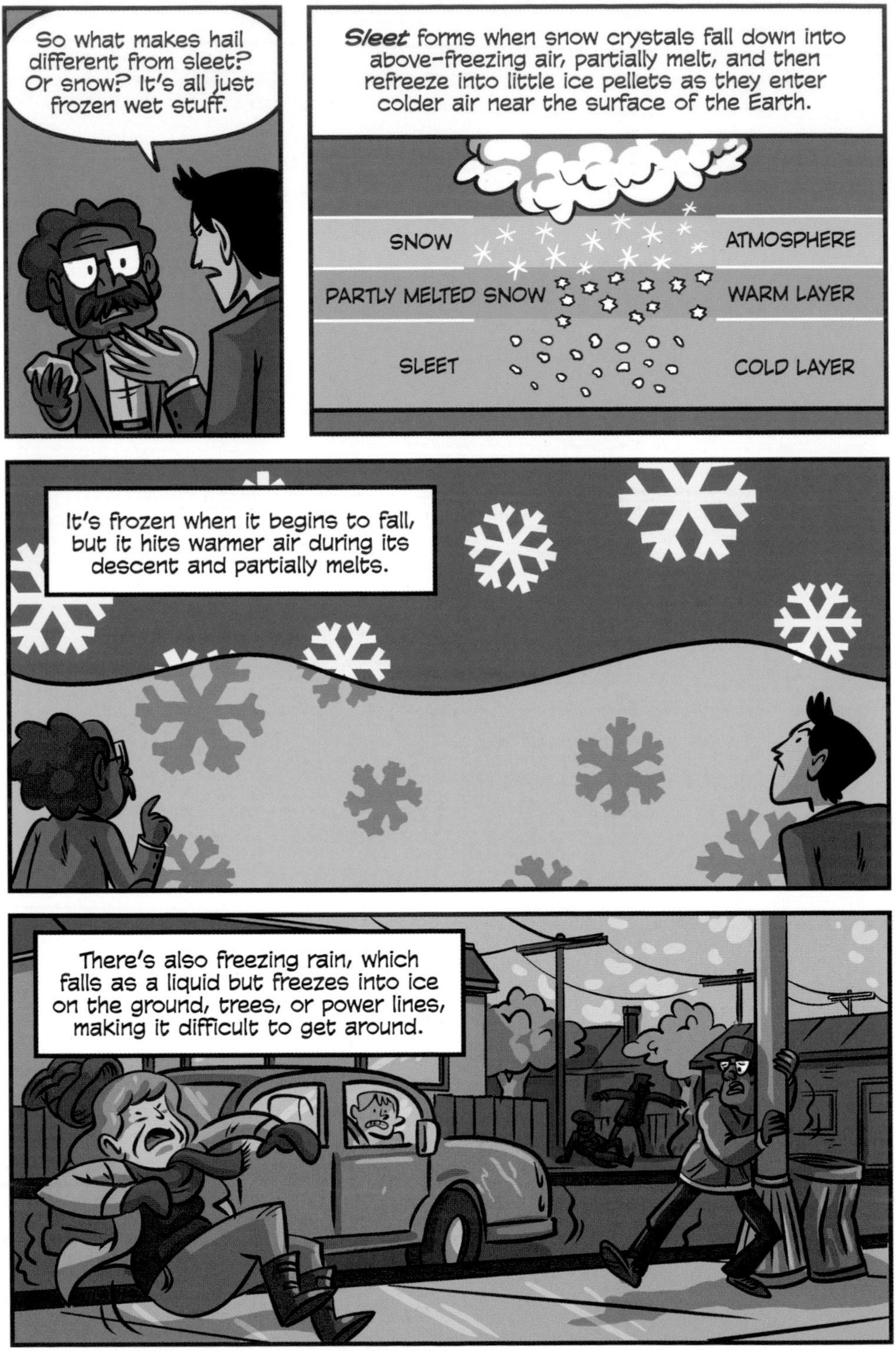

So what makes hail different from sleet? Or snow? It's all just frozen wet stuff.
Sleet forms when snow crystals fall down into above-freezing air, partially melt, and then refreeze into little ice pellets as they enter colder air near the surface of the Earth.
SNOW
ATMOSPHERE
PARTLY MELTED SNOW
WARM LAYER
SLEET
COLD LAYER
It's frozen when it begins to fall, but it hits warmer air during its descent and partially melts.
There's also freezing rain, which falls as a liquid but freezes into ice on the ground, trees, or power lines, making it difficult to get around.

76

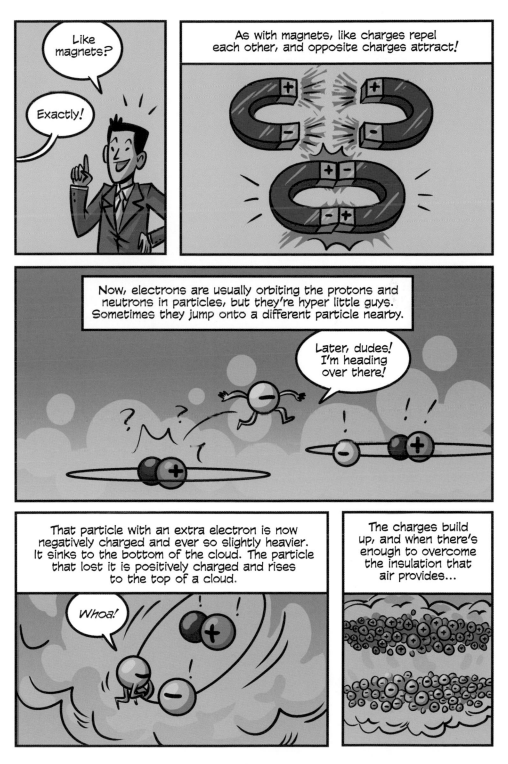

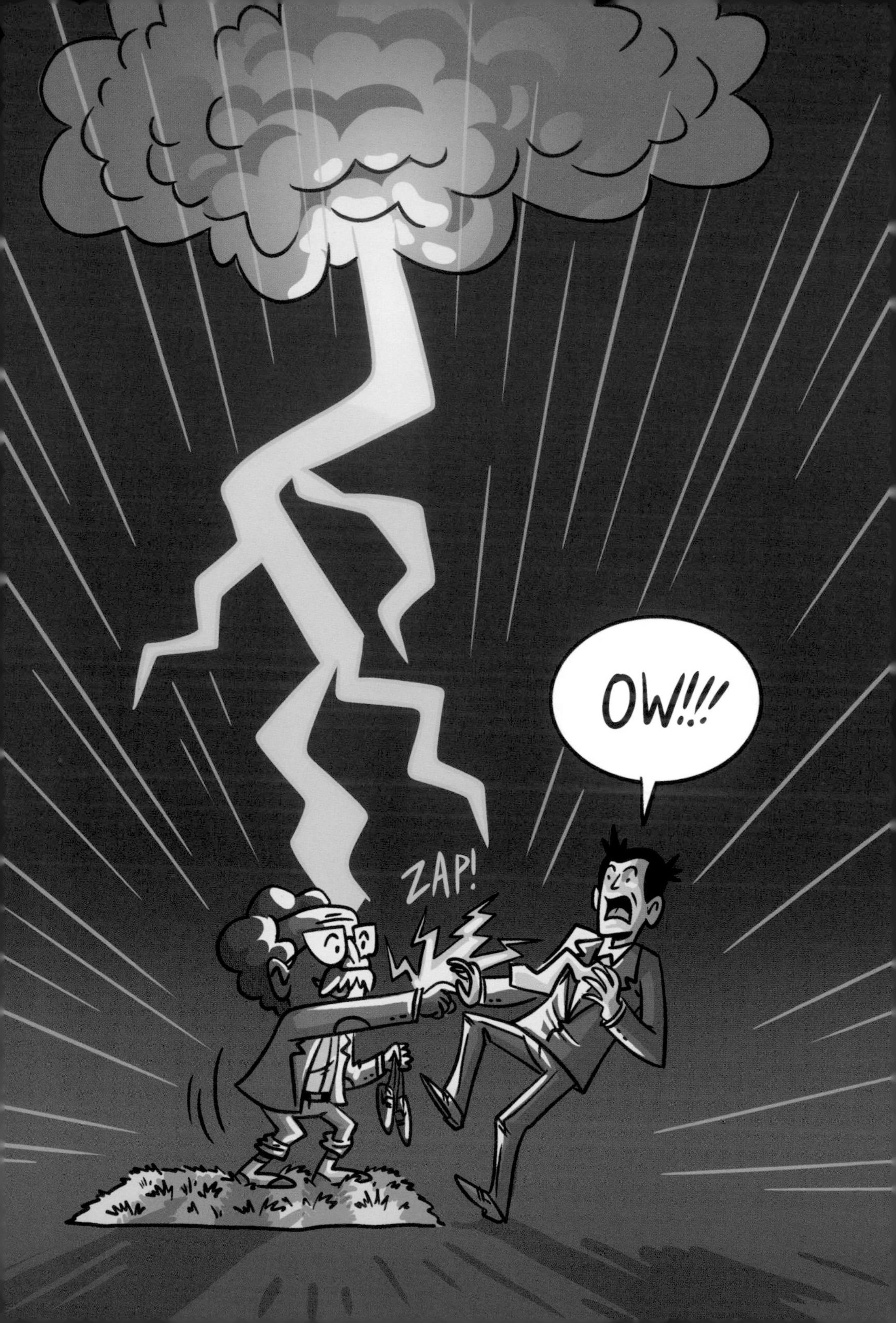
ZAP!
OW!!!

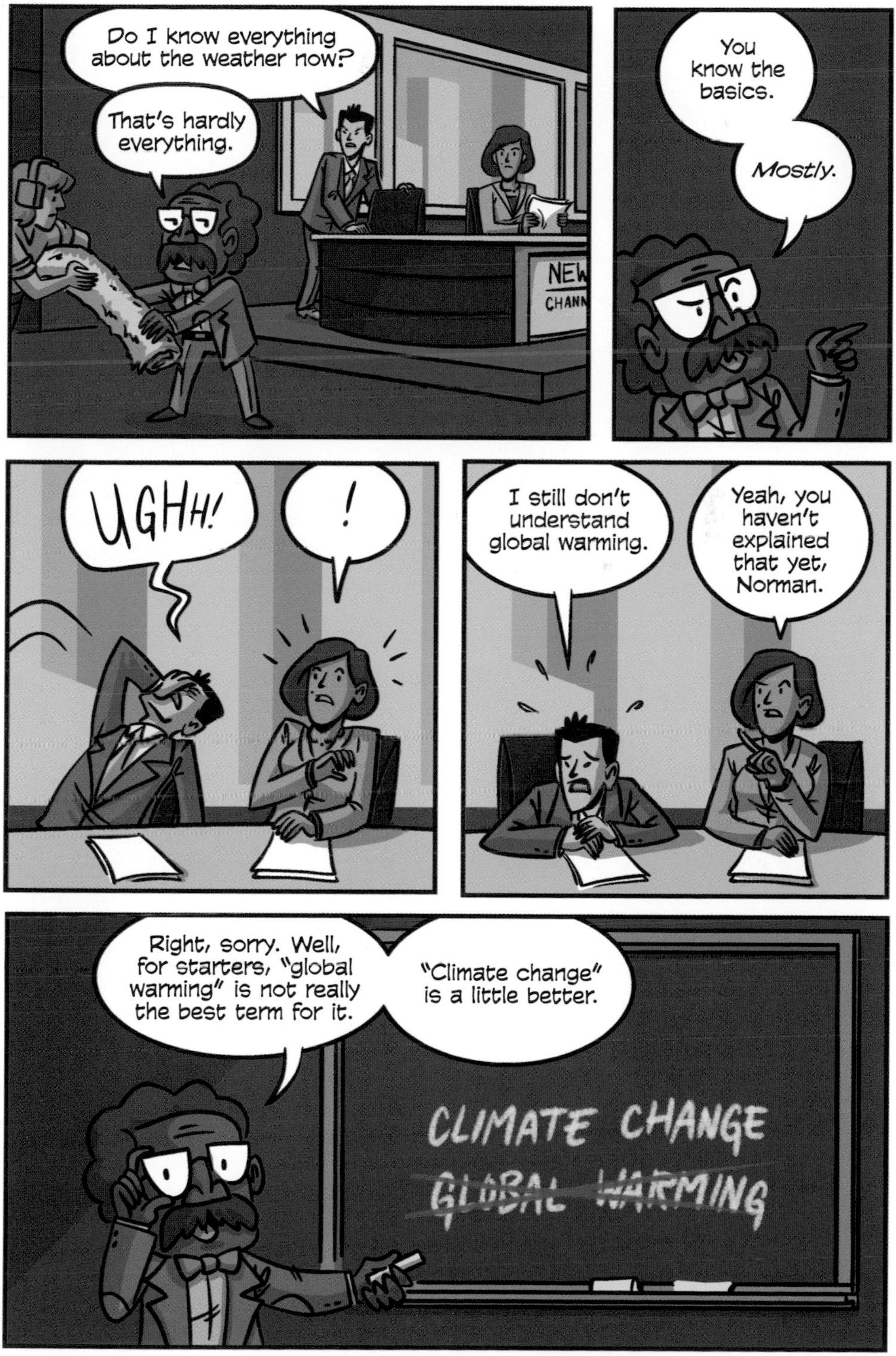

Do I know everything about the weather now?
That's hardly everything.
NEWS
CHANN
You know the basics.
Mostly.
UGHH!
!
I still don't understand global warming.
Yeah, you haven't explained that yet, Norman.
Right, sorry. Well, for starters, "global warming" is not really the best term for it.
"Climate change" is a little better.
CLIMATE CHANGE
~~GLOBAL WARMING~~

Day to day, the temperature changes a lot naturally. But we've been keeping detailed daily records of the weather across the globe for about 150 years.

We average the temperatures for a day over the entire globe and compare it against the previous averages. Over time, those averages have gone up, especially in recent years, raising the average temperature steadily higher.

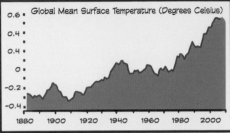

Global Mean Surface Temperature (Degrees Celsius)

Now, one hot day in winter doesn't always mean the end of the world, we know there are going to be variations. But several years of hotter-than-average temperatures, month after month, are a serious concern.

We know that human industries put chemicals into the atmosphere, which are trapping heat.

≥ cough ≤

We produce methane, which results from decomposition, such as garbage in a landfill. It's also a by-product of agriculture and livestock practices.

Carbon dioxide is a by-product of burning fossil fuels and of deforestation, so any time you drive or burn things for heat or fuel, it's created.

Well, in low-lying places near bodies of water, there are concerns about flooding because the ice and glaciers melting at the warmer polar regions is causing the ocean levels to rise.

And in other parts of the world, the warming is changing the weather patterns and causing droughts. When this happens, wildfires also tend to become more frequent.

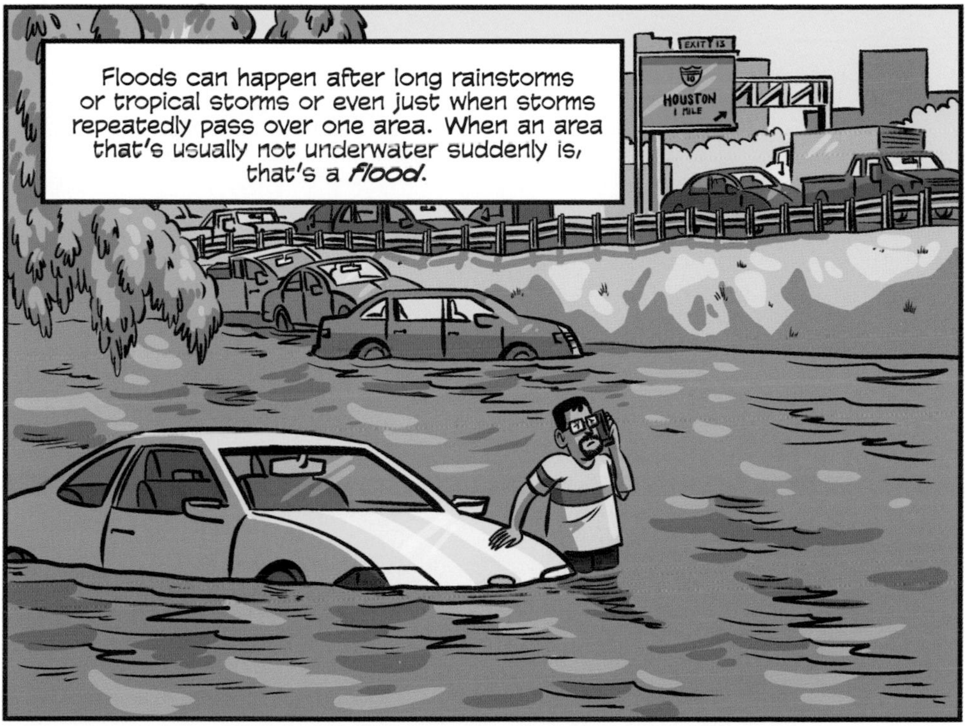
Floods can happen after long rainstorms or tropical storms or even just when storms repeatedly pass over one area. When an area that's usually not underwater suddenly is, that's a *flood*.
EXIT 13
HOUSTON
1 MILE

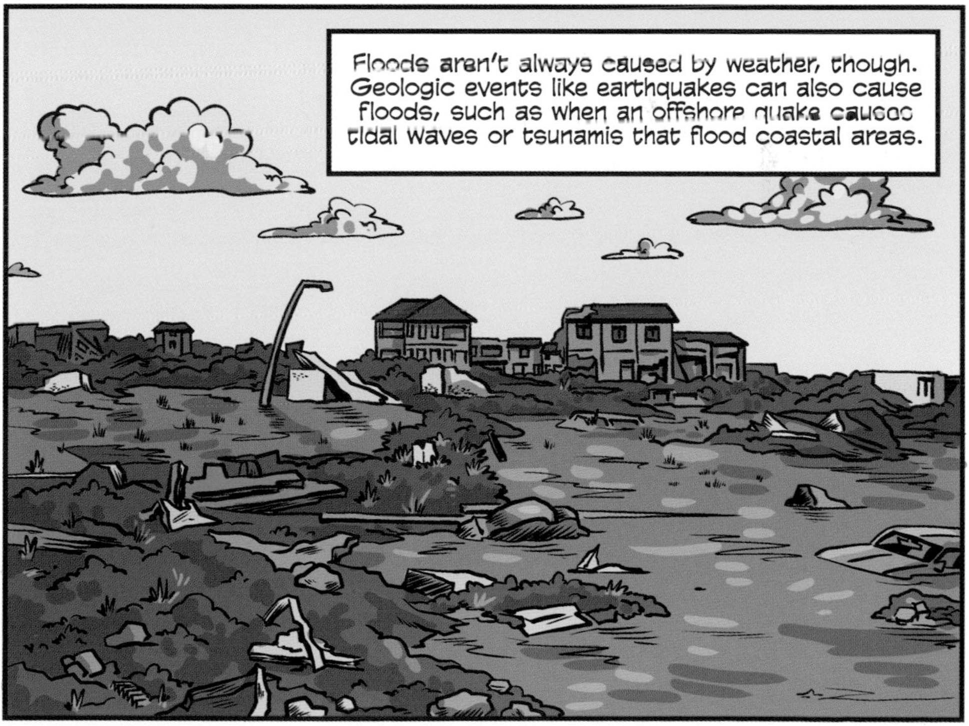
Floods aren't always caused by weather, though. Geologic events like earthquakes can also cause floods, such as when an offshore quake causes tidal waves or tsunamis that flood coastal areas.

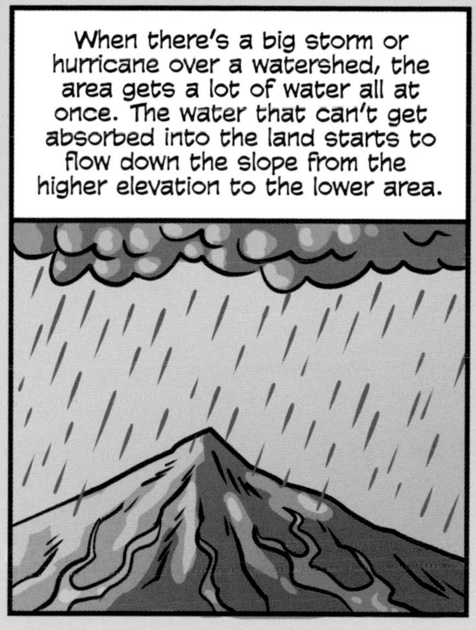
When there's a big storm or hurricane over a watershed, the area gets a lot of water all at once. The water that can't get absorbed into the land starts to flow down the slope from the higher elevation to the lower area.

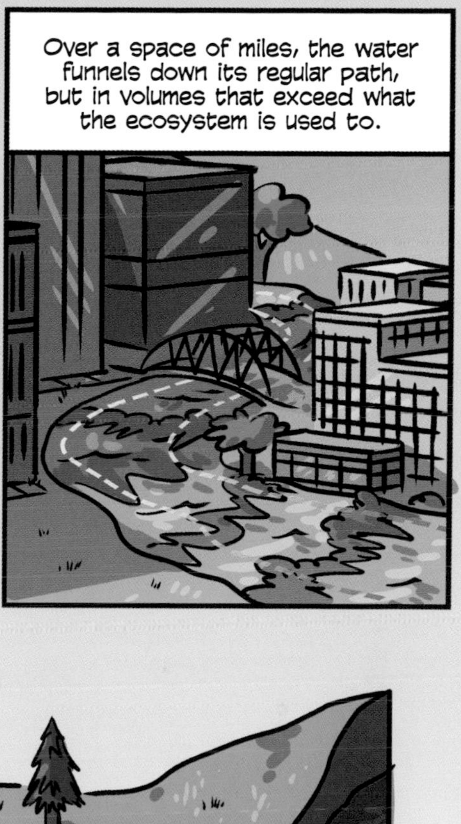
Over a space of miles, the water funnels down its regular path, but in volumes that exceed what the ecosystem is used to.

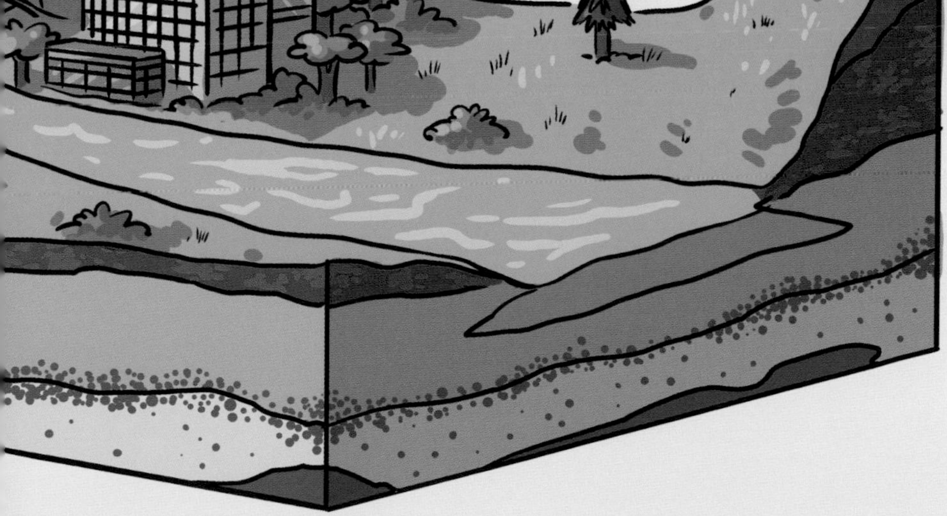

The unusually large volume of water erodes away land, picks up debris, and even knocks over massive trees, further changing the previous directions of the flow of the water and complicating the situation.

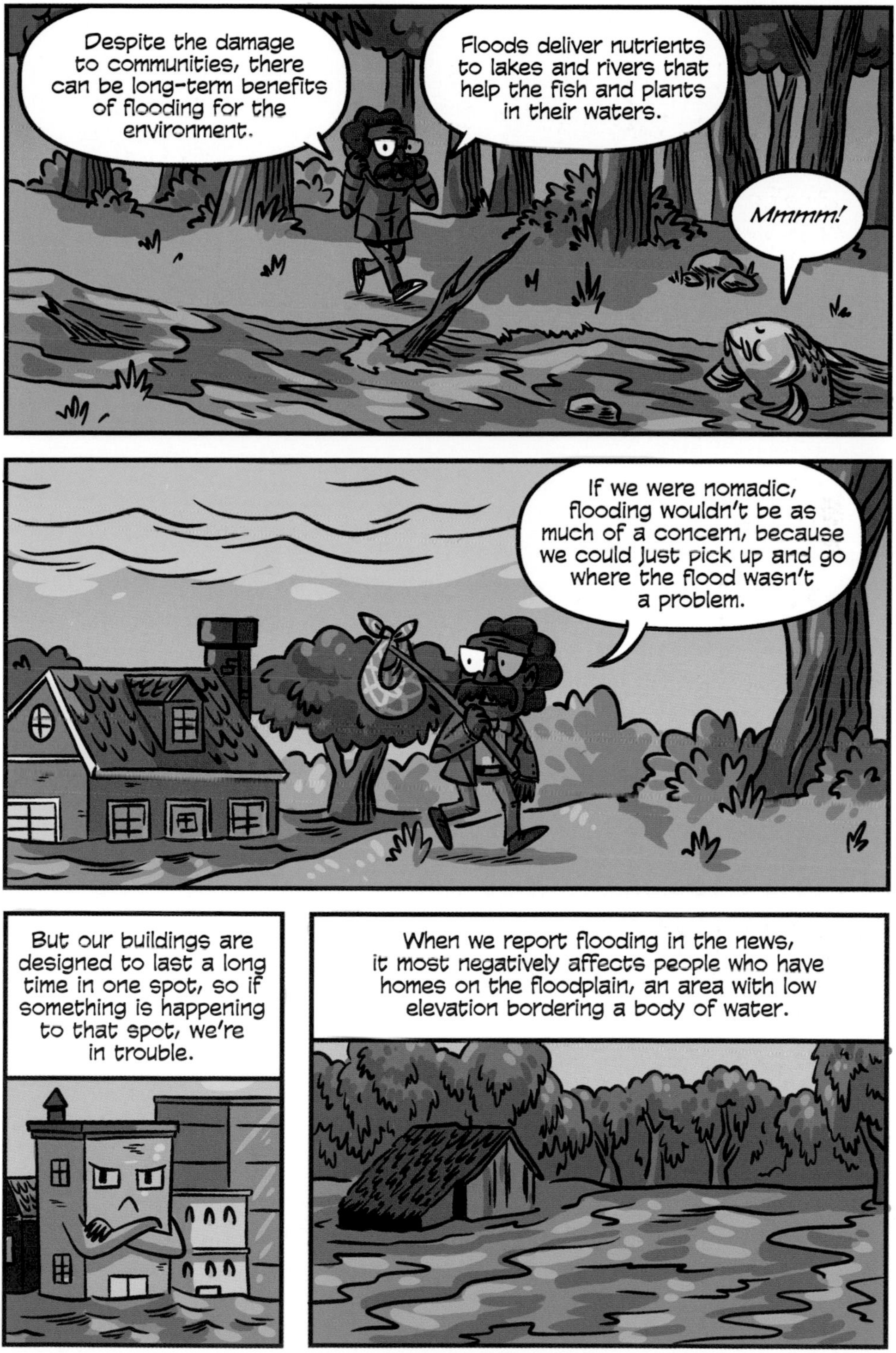
Despite the damage to communities, there can be long-term benefits of flooding for the environment.
Floods deliver nutrients to lakes and rivers that help the fish and plants in their waters.
Mmmm!
If we were nomadic, flooding wouldn't be as much of a concern, because we could just pick up and go where the flood wasn't a problem.
But our buildings are designed to last a long time in one spot, so if something is happening to that spot, we're in trouble.
When we report flooding in the news, it most negatively affects people who have homes on the floodplain, an area with low elevation bordering a body of water.

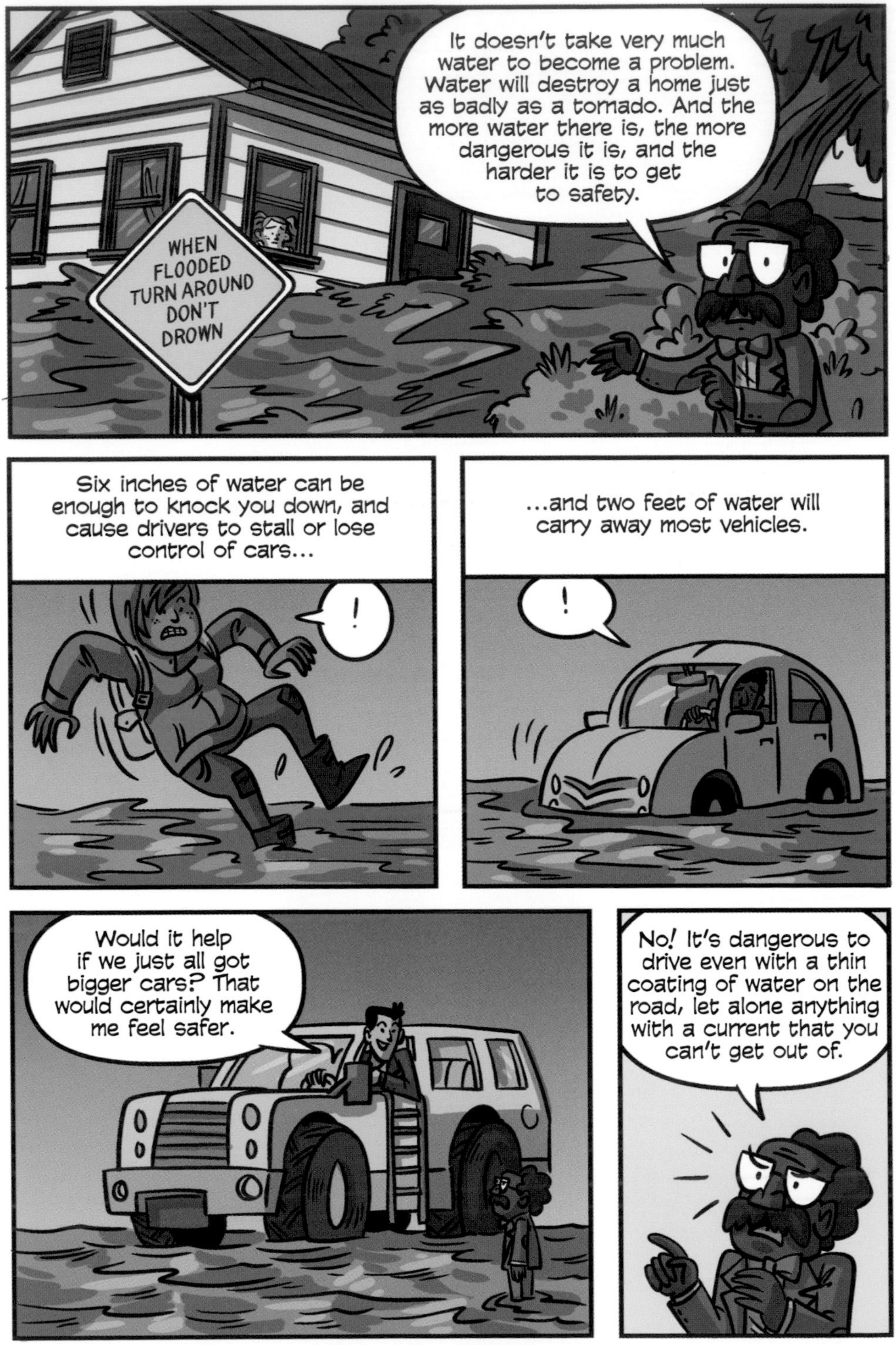

It doesn't take very much water to become a problem. Water will destroy a home just as badly as a tornado. And the more water there is, the more dangerous it is, and the harder it is to get to safety.
WHEN FLOODED TURN AROUND DON'T DROWN
Six inches of water can be enough to knock you down, and cause drivers to stall or lose control of cars...
!
...and two feet of water will carry away most vehicles.
!
Would it help if we just all got bigger cars? That would certainly make me feel safer.
No! It's dangerous to drive even with a thin coating of water on the road, let alone anything with a current that you can't get out of.

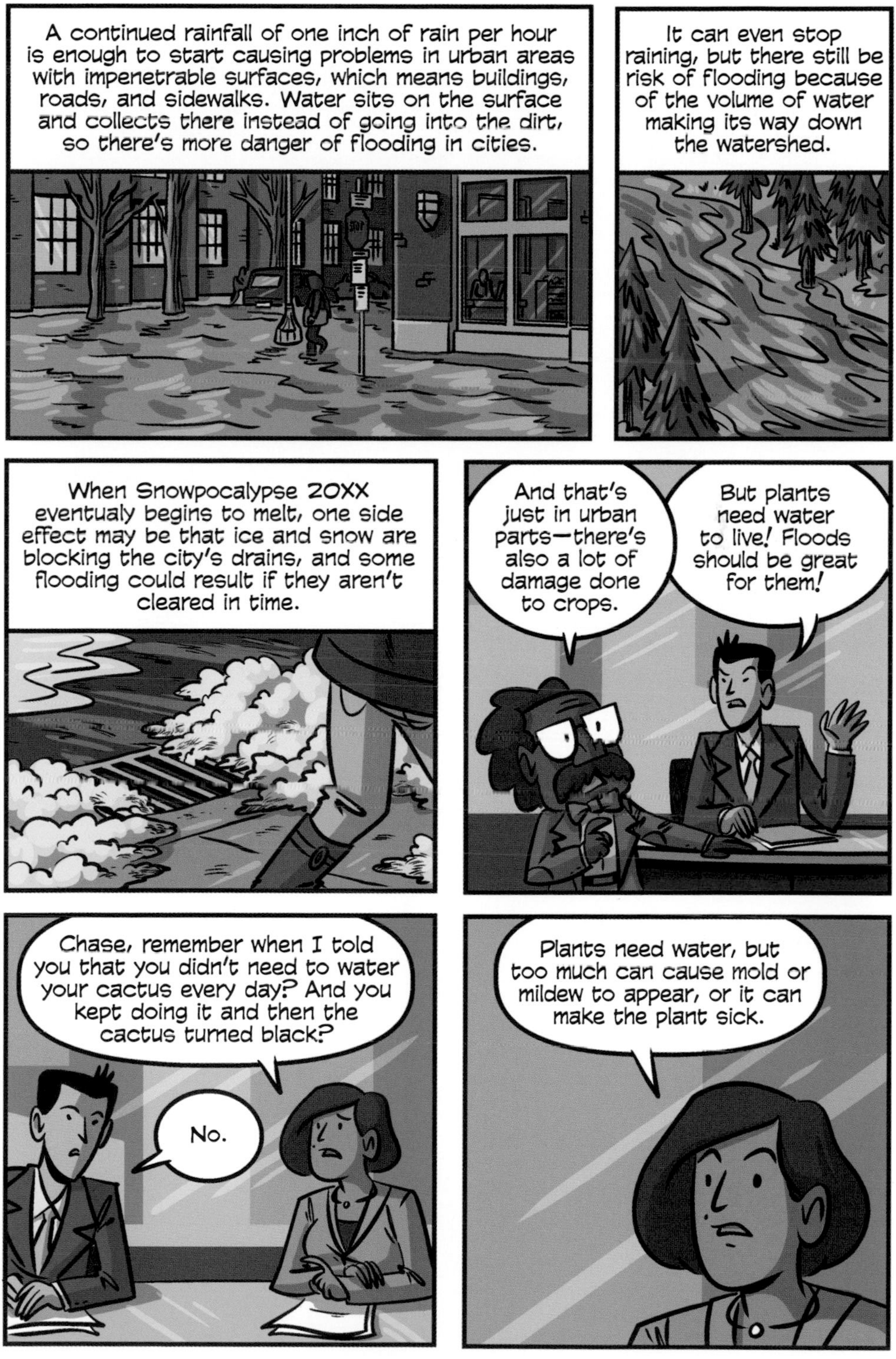
A continued rainfall of one inch of rain per hour is enough to start causing problems in urban areas with impenetrable surfaces, which means buildings, roads, and sidewalks. Water sits on the surface and collects there instead of going into the dirt, so there's more danger of flooding in cities.
It can even stop raining, but there still be risk of flooding because of the volume of water making its way down the watershed.
When Snowpocalypse 20XX eventualy begins to melt, one side effect may be that ice and snow are blocking the city's drains, and some flooding could result if they aren't cleared in time.
And that's just in urban parts—there's also a lot of damage done to crops.
But plants need water to live! Floods should be great for them!
Chase, remember when I told you that you didn't need to water your cactus every day? And you kept doing it and then the cactus turned black?
No.
Plants need water, but too much can cause mold or mildew to appear, or it can make the plant sick.

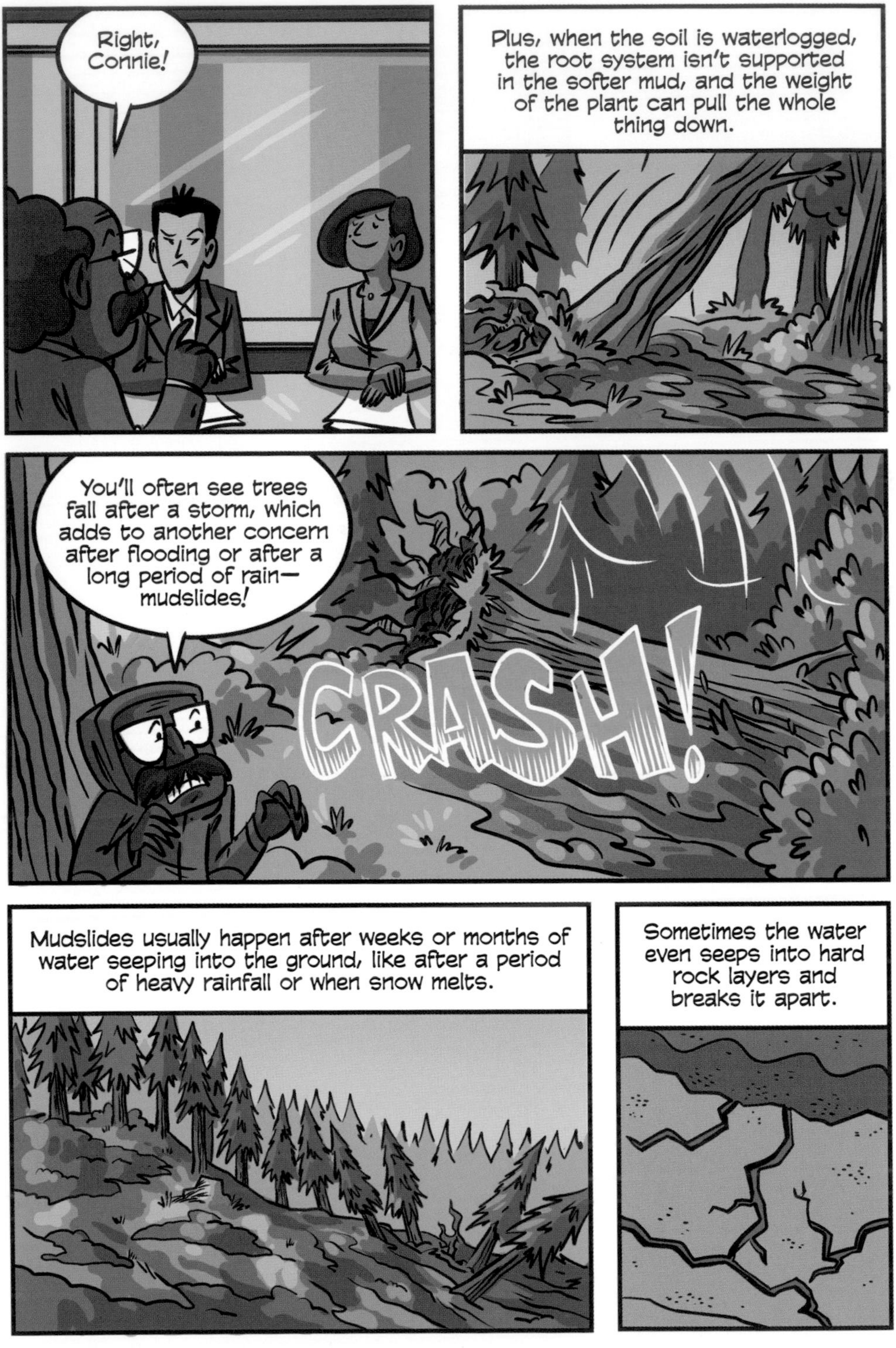
Right, Connie!
Plus, when the soil is waterlogged, the root system isn't supported in the softer mud, and the weight of the plant can pull the whole thing down.
You'll often see trees fall after a storm, which adds to another concern after flooding or after a long period of rain—mudslides!
CRASH!
Mudslides usually happen after weeks or months of water seeping into the ground, like after a period of heavy rainfall or when snow melts.
Sometimes the water even seeps into hard rock layers and breaks it apart.

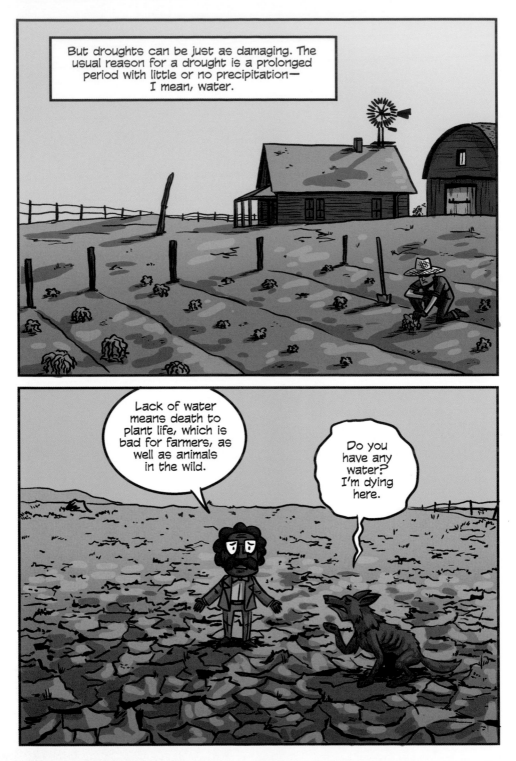

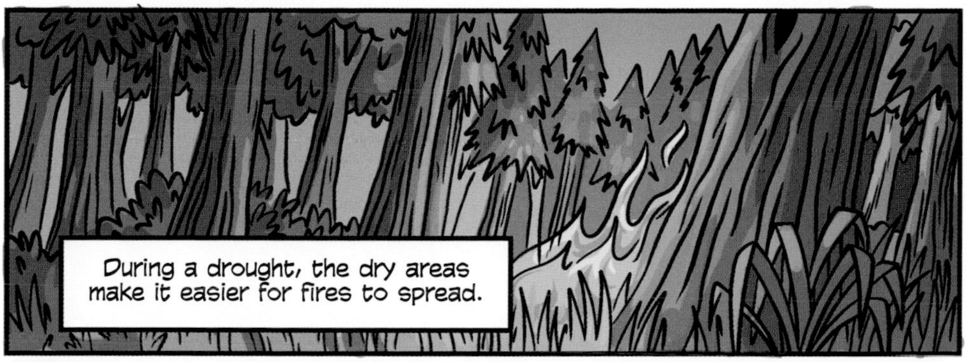
During a drought, the dry areas make it easier for fires to spread.

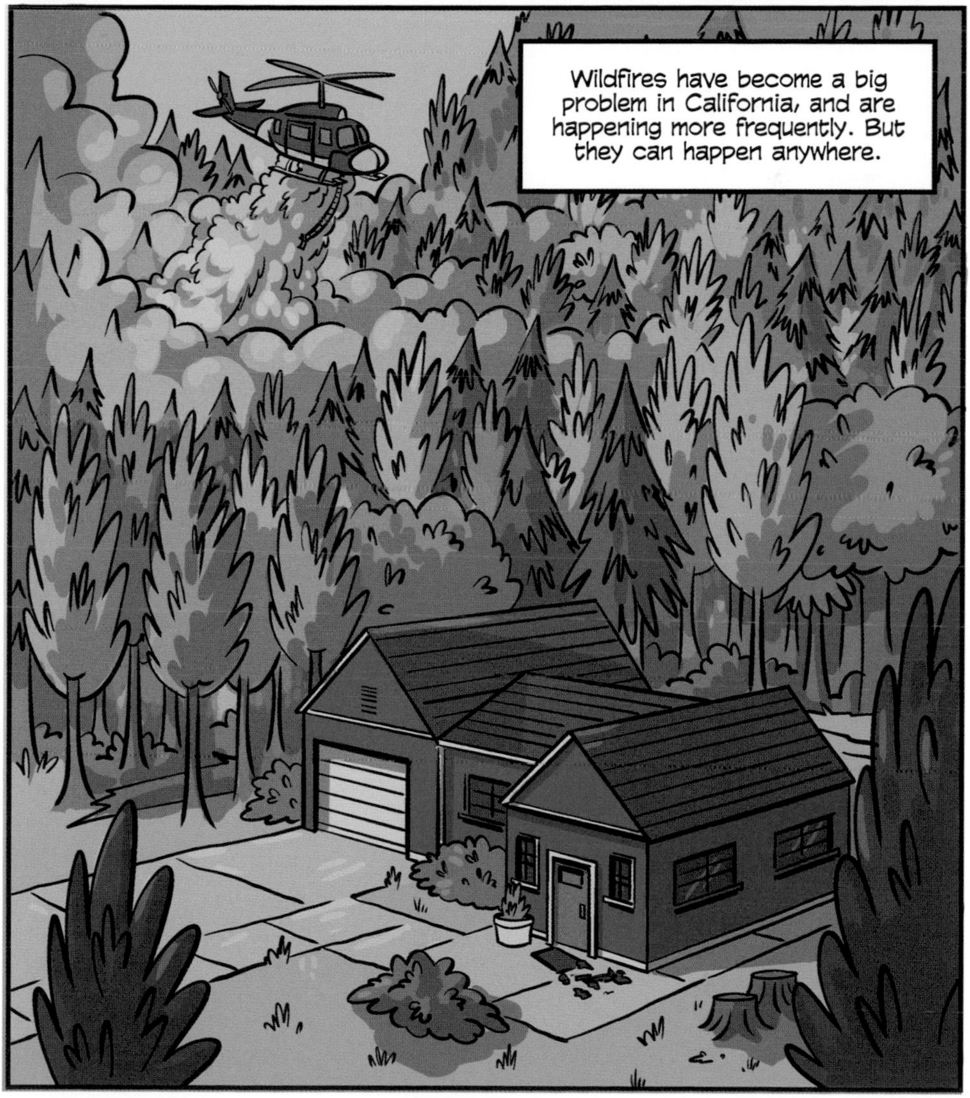
Wildfires have become a big problem in California, and are happening more frequently. But they can happen anywhere.

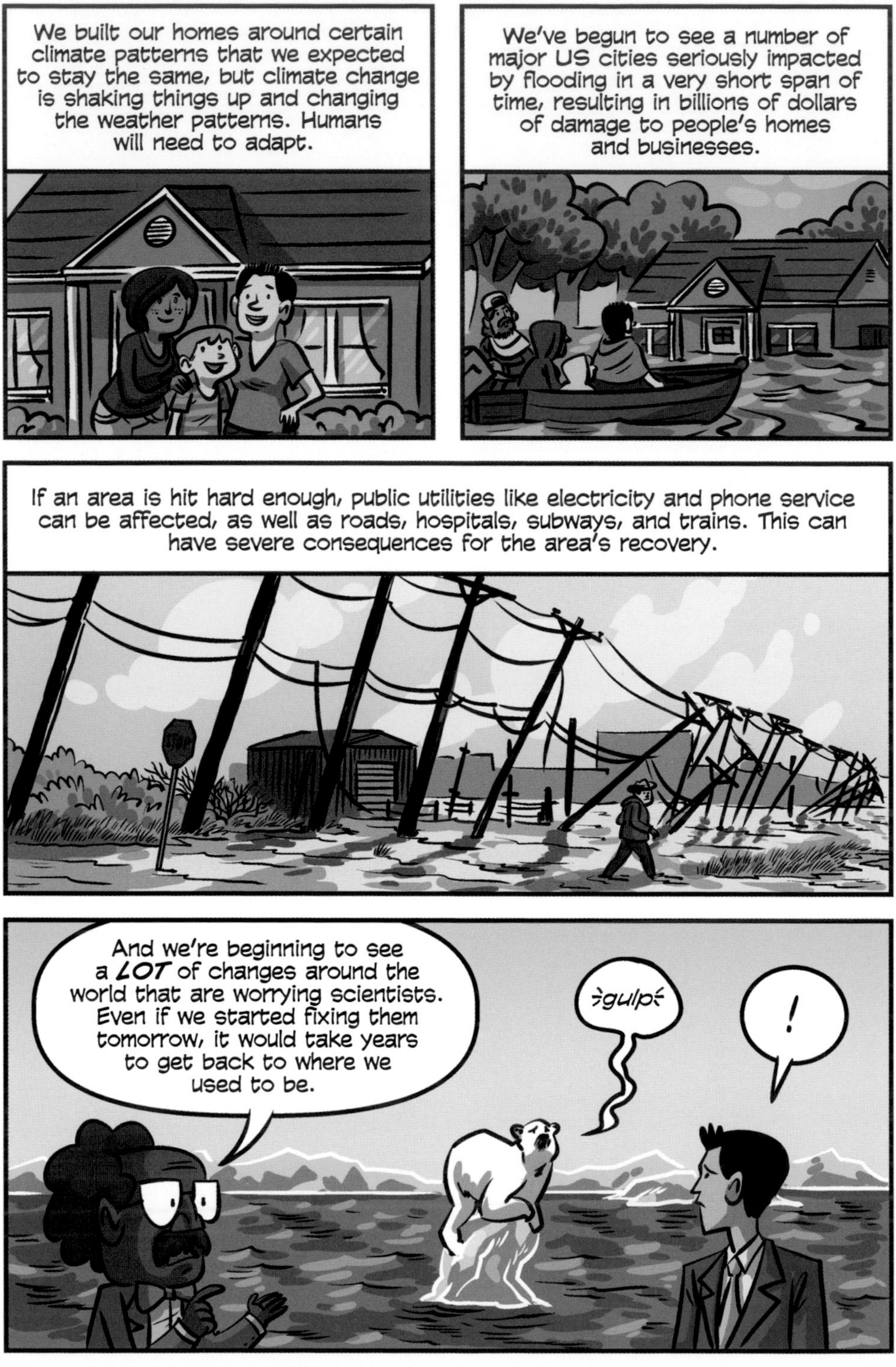
We built our homes around certain climate patterns that we expected to stay the same, but climate change is shaking things up and changing the weather patterns. Humans will need to adapt.
We've begun to see a number of major US cities seriously impacted by flooding in a very short span of time, resulting in billions of dollars of damage to people's homes and businesses.
If an area is hit hard enough, public utilities like electricity and phone service can be affected, as well as roads, hospitals, subways, and trains. This can have severe consequences for the area's recovery.
And we're beginning to see a *LOT* of changes around the world that are worrying scientists. Even if we started fixing them tomorrow, it would take years to get back to where we used to be.
gulp
!

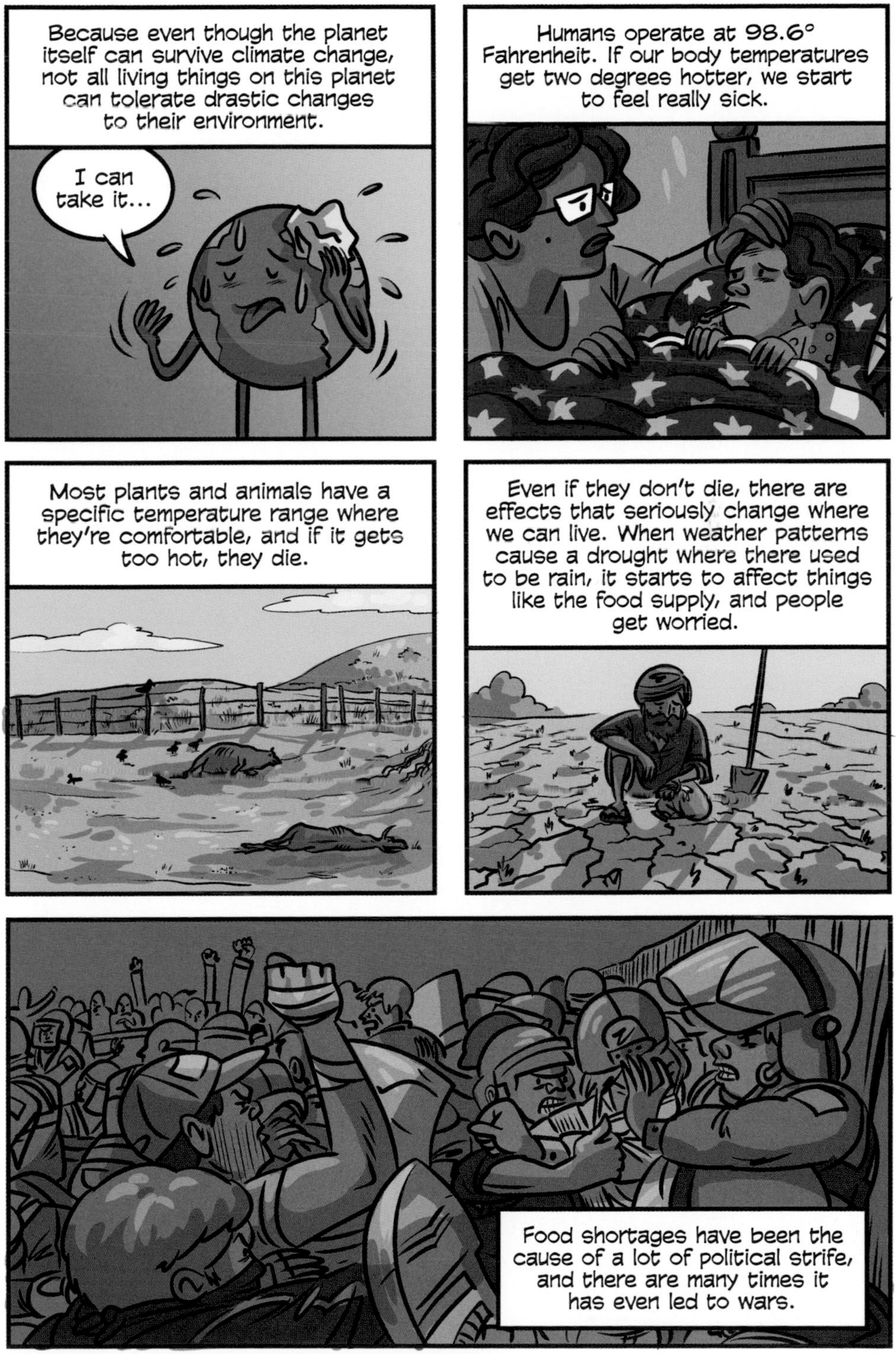
Because even though the planet itself can survive climate change, not all living things on this planet can tolerate drastic changes to their environment.
I can take it...
Humans operate at 98.6° Fahrenheit. If our body temperatures get two degrees hotter, we start to feel really sick.
Most plants and animals have a specific temperature range where they're comfortable, and if it gets too hot, they die.
Even if they don't die, there are effects that seriously change where we can live. When weather patterns cause a drought where there used to be rain, it starts to affect things like the food supply, and people get worried.
Food shortages have been the cause of a lot of political strife, and there are many times it has even led to wars.

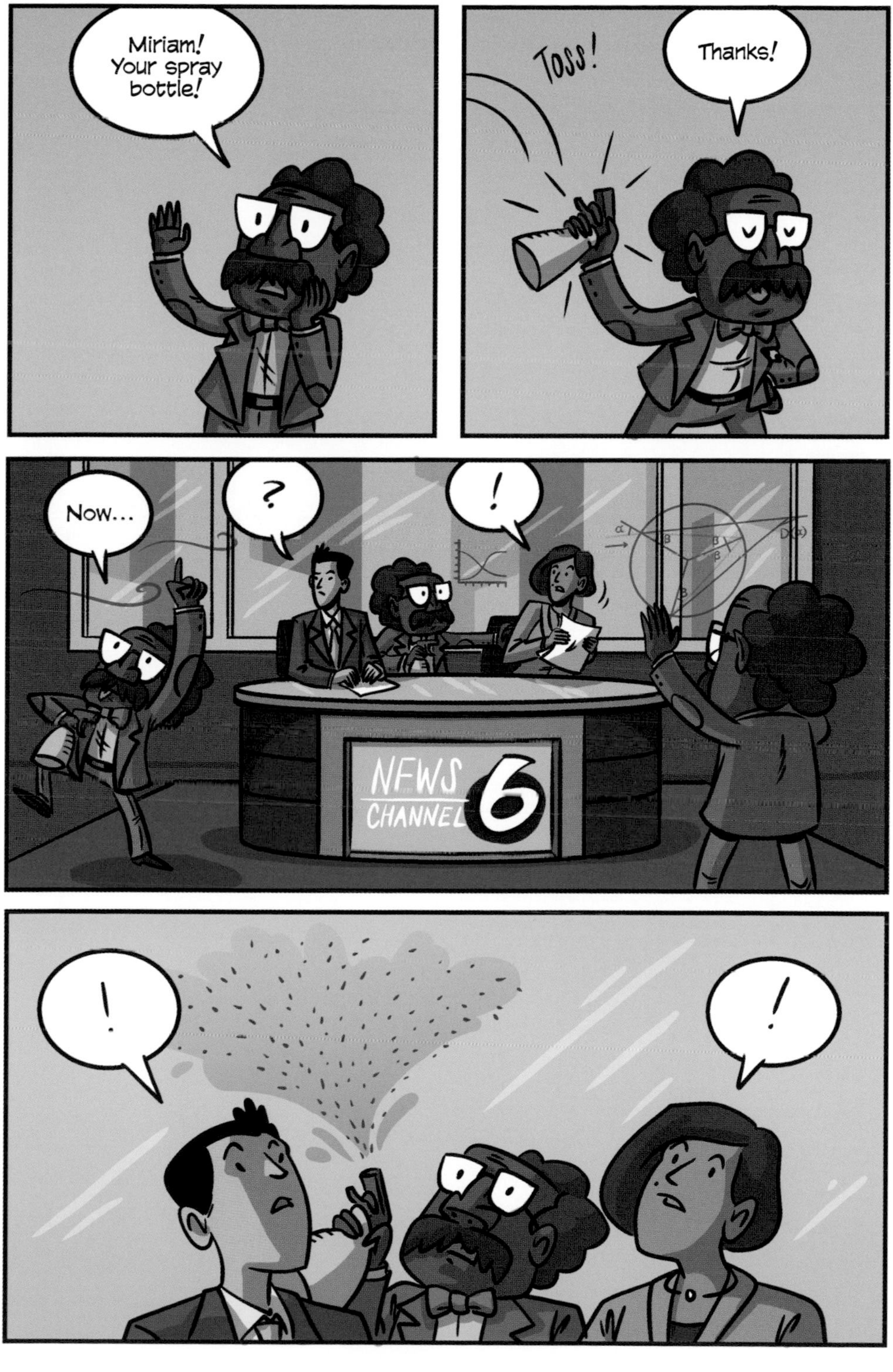
Miriam! Your spray bottle!
TOSS!
Thanks!
Now...
?
!
NEWS
CHANNEL 6
!
!

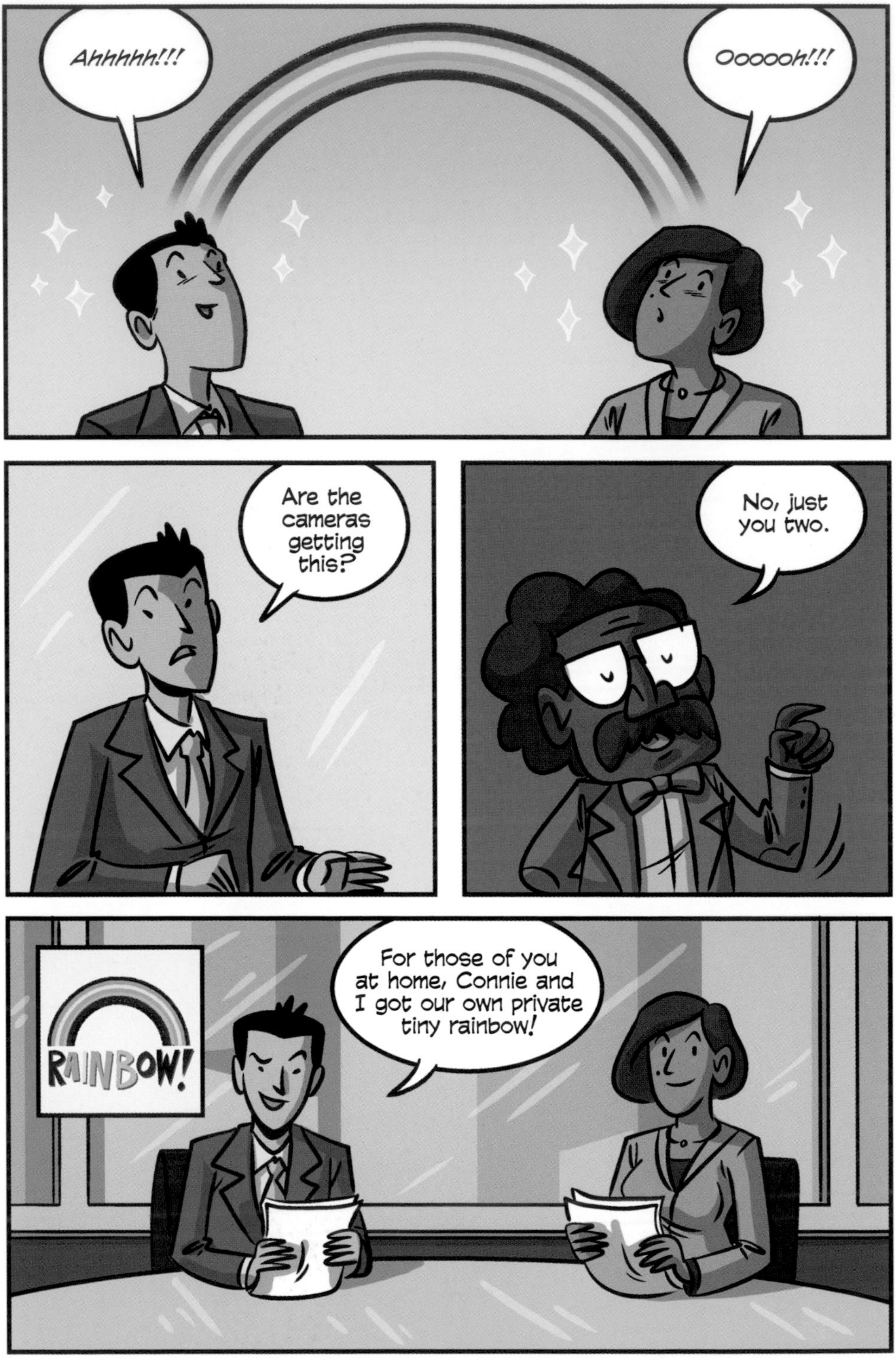
Ahhhhh!!!
Oooooh!!!
Are the cameras getting this?
No, just you two.
RAINBOW!
For those of you at home, Connie and I got our own private tiny rainbow!

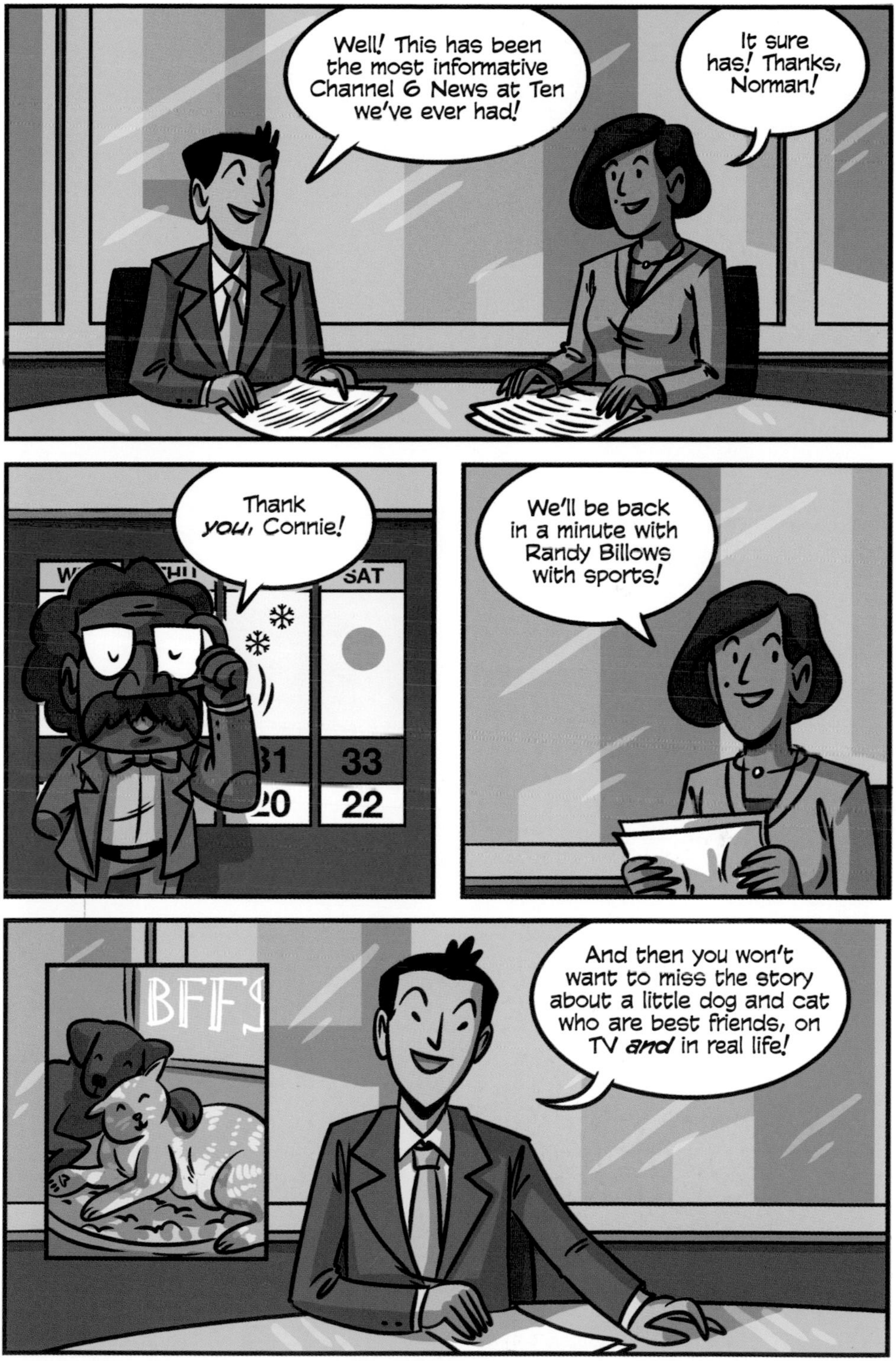
Well! This has been the most informative Channel 6 News at Ten we've ever had!
It sure has! Thanks, Norman!
Thank *you*, Connie!
SAT
33
22
We'll be back in a minute with Randy Billows with sports!
BFFS
And then you won't want to miss the story about a little dog and cat who are best friends, on TV *and* in real life!

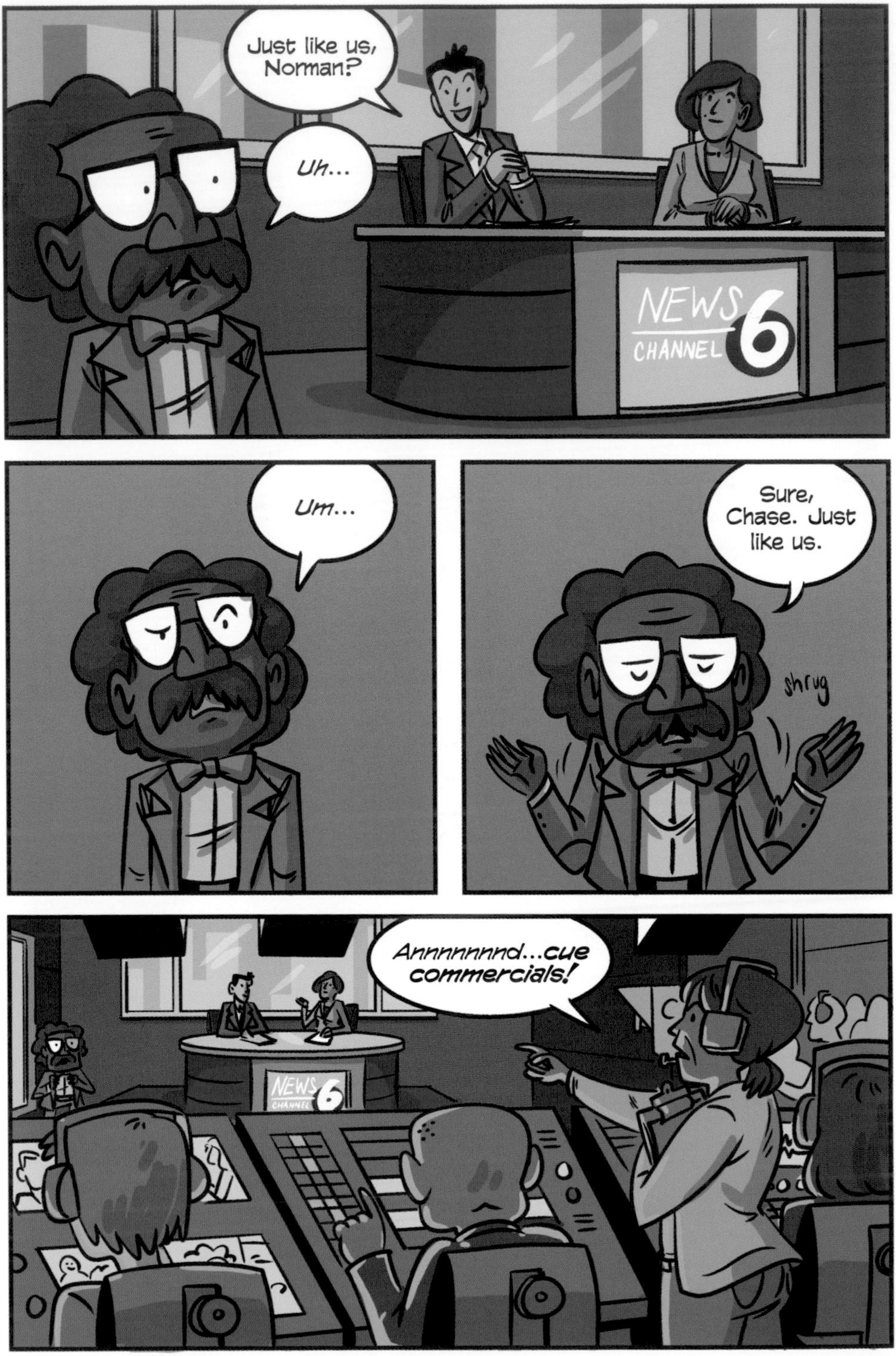

Just like us, Norman?
Uh...
Um...
Sure, Chase. Just like us.
shrug
Annnnnnd...cue commercials!
NEWS CHANNEL 6

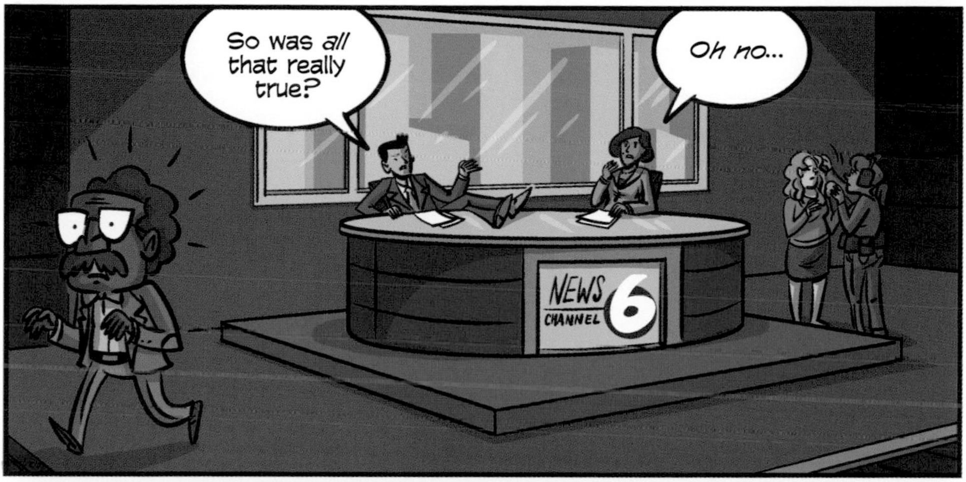
So was *all* that really true?
Oh no...

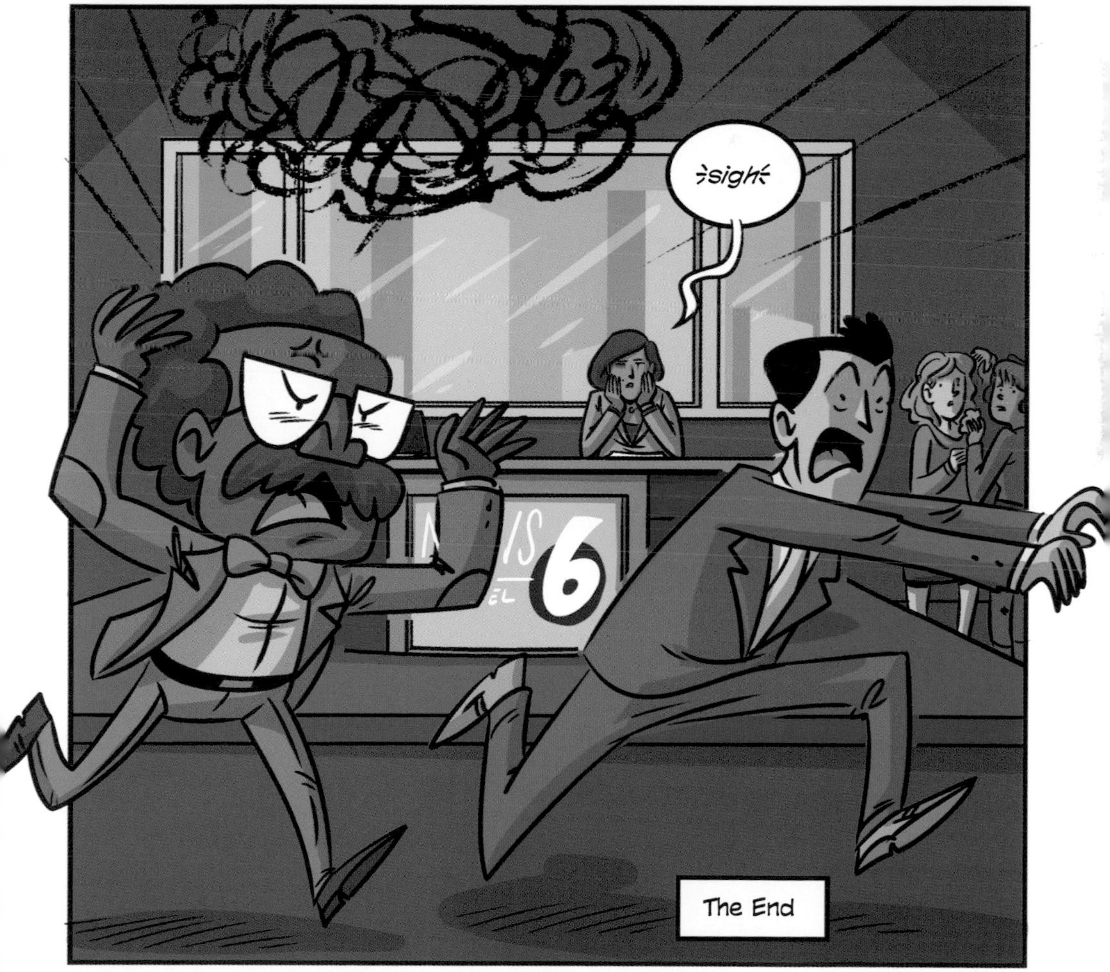
sigh
The End

—GLOSSARY—

Atmosphere
The layers of gas surrounding a planet between the surface and outer space.

Axis
An imaginary line on which a sphere rotates.

Carbon footprint
The amount of carbon dioxide or carbon compounds emitted due to the fossil fuels made in the production of materials used by a person or group.

Circulation
The movement of a fluid or gas within a contained space or back and forth around an area.

Celsius
The standard scientific unit of measurement for temperature.

Climate
The general weather conditions in an area over a period of time.

Condensation
When a vapor or gas becomes a liquid.

Crystallize
When a substance hardens into a rigid solid form.

Drought
A period of time without rain that is longer than average for an area.

Ecosystem
A community of interacting organisms and their environment.

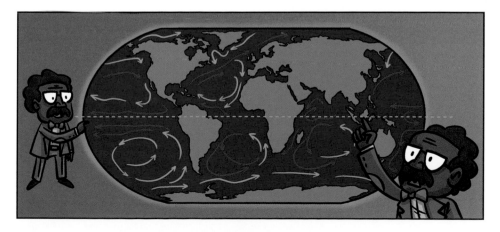

—GLOSSARY CONTINUED—

Environment
   The surroundings that a person or living thing exist in.

Erosion
   Gradually wearing away or destroying something over a length of time.

Evaporation
   The process through which liquid water becomes a gas.

Fahrenheit
   The US standard unit of measurement for temperature.

Floodplain
   An area where flooding regularly occurs.

Granules
   Small units of substance, such as grains.

Hemisphere
   One half of a sphere, or one half of the planet.

Meteorology
   The study of weather.

Polar
   Having to do with the North or South Pole.

Precipitation
   Moisture condensed from water vapor, which falls to the earth.

Rotate
>   To move in a set path around an axis, to revolve.

Sphere
>   Shaped like a round ball.

Thermometer
>   A device that measures temperature.

Transpiration
>   The process through which a plant releases water vapor.

Updraft
>   An upward current of air.

Urban
>   Relating to a city.

Vapor
>   A substance diffused in the air or a gas.

Virga
>   Rain that evaporates before it hits the ground.

Watershed
>   An area of land that drains streams and rainfall to a common outlet such as a reservoir, basin, or mouth of a bay.

Weather
>   The daily conditions of the atmosphere, regarding heat, humidity, wind, precipitation, and cloud conditions.

—WEATHER TOOLS—

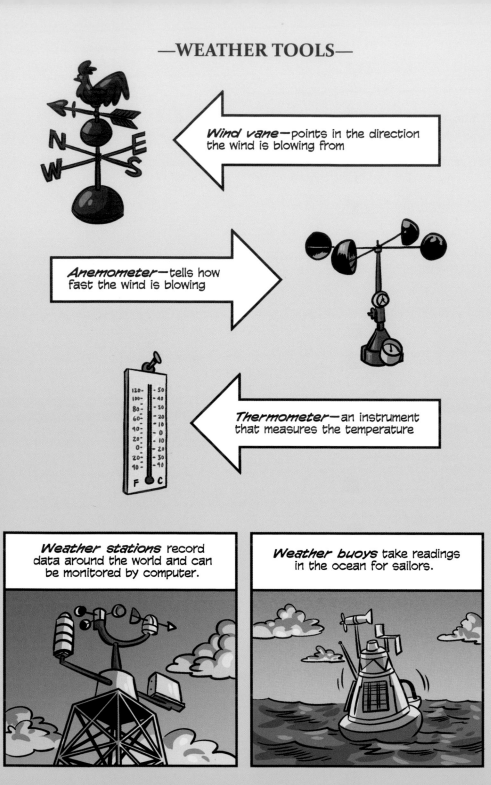

Wind vane—points in the direction the wind is blowing from

Anemometer—tells how fast the wind is blowing

Thermometer—an instrument that measures the temperature

Weather stations record data around the world and can be monitored by computer.

Weather buoys take readings in the ocean for sailors.

Hygrometer—an instrument that measures the water vapor content of the atmosphere

Rain gauge—collects the rain and tells how much has fallen at a certain location

Barometer—measures the atmospheric pressure

Radar can show us what's happening in the clouds.

Satellites can take readings from space on temperature, wind, and humidity, and give us details about clouds and their movements.

—WILD WEATHER MYTHS: DEBUNKED!—

by Alicia Wasula, consulting meteorologist

Is the air really "too heavy" to hit home runs on humid days?

No! Humid air contains a lot of water vapor, which is less dense than some of the other gasses in the atmosphere. So actually, it is theoretically possible to hit more home runs on humid days than on dry days. However, elevation matters too. Ball parks at high altitudes with thinner atmosphere, such as Coors Field, where the Colorado Rockies play, see more home runs hit than at other ball parks.

Is a car a safe place to be during a thunderstorm?

Yes, but maybe not for the reason you might expect. Many people learn that the rubber in the tires acts as an insulation against lightning striking the car. In fact, the metal frame of the car acts like what is known as a "Faraday cage," essentially keeping all of the electrical current on the outside of the car. So as long as you're not touching metal parts of the frame, you are safe from lightning strikes inside your car.

Do "pure" raindrops exist?

No! Every cloud and raindrop forms on a surface, known as a nucleus. Nuclei can be tiny solid particles such as dust, sea salt, sand, or even tiny bugs!

Does the cone of uncertainty represent the size of the hurricane?

No! The "cone of uncertainty" forecast, like the one shown for Hurricane Maria (2017) here, represents the range of potential tracks that the storm center may follow. The further out the forecast is in time, the wider the cone, or the larger the range in possible tracks. It is possible to experience effects of the storm even outside of the cone because a hurricane's effects can extend out from the center of the track.

35 N
30 N
25 N
20 N
15 N
10 N
90 W
85 W
80 W
75 W
70 W
65 W
60 W
55 W
50 W
45 W
2 PM Sat
2 PM Fri
2 AM Wed
5 PM Mon
2 PM Thu
2 PM Wed
2 PM Tue

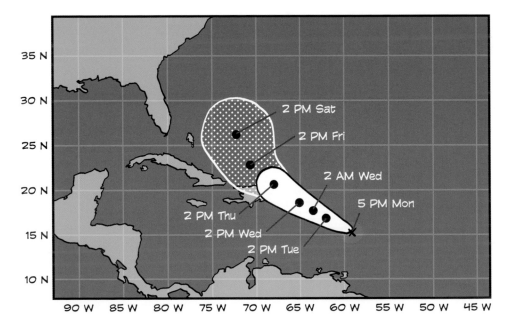

Should I open my windows during a tornado to equalize the pressure inside my house?

Absolutely not! By opening your windows during a tornado or other windstorm, you allow flying debris to enter your house and potentially injure the people inside. During a tornado, the safest place to be is in a windowless room toward the interior of the house.

Can cows predict rain?

Maybe, but it is hard to tell for sure because cows lie down for many reasons (like people!) and they cannot tell us why.

Are double rainbows identical to each other?

When you see a double rainbow, the inner rainbow has the more common color arrangement of red on the outside, orange, yellow, green, blue, and violet on the inside. In the less commonly seen outer arc, the colors are in reverse order so that violet will appear on the outside of the rainbow!

My soccer coach said that it is more dangerous to play in a dry heat than in a humid heat. Is this correct?

Your coach is right! On a dry day, your sweat evaporates much more readily from your skin than on a humid day, so it is possible to lose more fluids if you don't drink enough. However, on a humid day your sweat doesn't evaporate as efficiently, so it is still possible to overheat. The bottom line: if it's a hot day, make sure to hydrate well and take breaks if you are outside.

—WILD WEATHER MYTHS: CONTINUED!—

My dad put salt on our icy driveway and told me that it would melt the ice. How does this happen?

Actually, salt does not technically "melt" ice. When put on icy pavement, salt slowly dissolves into the ice, creating a salty solution. The freezing point of salt water is lower than the freezing point of plain water (32 degrees Fahrenheit), and so the ice that would have been frozen at 32 degrees can remain liquid at much colder temperatures than if no salt had been used.

Can lightning strike the same place twice?

Although popular belief would say that "lightning can't strike the same place twice," this is really not true. Tall locations are particularly prone to repeated lightning strikes. The Empire State Building, in New York City, has been struck by lightning many times over the years!

Do raindrops really look like teardrops when they fall?

Surprisingly, this is not the most aerodynamic shape that liquid raindrops take when they fall down to the ground. As a drop falls, the air resistance pushes upward on the center of the drop, which then assumes a hamburger-bun-like shape. Eventually the force becomes large enough that the drop can break apart into smaller drops, and the process repeats.

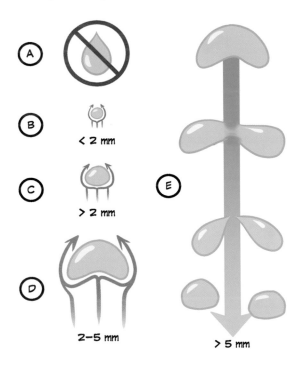

Different sizes of raindrops:

A) Raindrops are not tear-shaped, as most people think.

B) Very small raindrops are almost spherical in shape.

C) Larger raindrops become flattened at the bottom, like that of a hamburger bun, due to air resistance.

D) Large raindrops have a large amount of air resistance, which makes them begin to become unstable.

E) Very large raindrops split into smaller raindrops due to air resistance.

A) 〇

B) < 2 mm

C) > 2 mm

D) 2–5 mm

E) > 5 mm